Foreword by
Michael L. Brown PhD

The Way to Victory Over Idolatry

CHARLES SIMPSON

BRIDGE LOGOS

Newberry, FL 32669

Bridge-Logos
Newberry, FL 32669

Knowing El Kanna Our Jealous God:
The Way to Victory Over Idolatry
by Charles Simpson

Printed in the United States of America.

Library of Congress Catalog Card Number: 2023949499

International Standard Book Number: 978-1-61036-499-7

Cover and interior design/layout:
Ashley Morgan | GraphicGardenLLC@gmail.com

VP 02/2024

Dedication

I dedicate this book to Don Wilkerson who gave me the encouragement I needed to launch my first and fifth church plants, and a lot of things in between! Your constant encouragement, wisdom, strength, and humor have blessed thousands of lives, and I'm very thankful Brother Don that I'm one of them! I also gratefully acknowledge the encouragement and support of Don and Georgette Meggelin as well as Chris and Mary Ann (Peluso) McGahan.

Contents

PART ONE

THE PROPHETS KNEW GOD'S JEALOUSY

PART TWO

HE'S JEALOUS OVER OUR IDOLATRY

PART THREE
THE TRANSFORMATION OF ISRAEL, AND US

PART FOUR
A GLORIOUS, VICTORIOUS CHURCH

Foreword

We are all familiar with these words from the Ten Commandments:

> You shall not make for yourself an image in the form of anything in heaven above or on the earth beneath or in the waters below. You shall not bow down to them or worship them; for I, the LORD your God, am a jealous God, punishing the children for the sin of the parents to the third and fourth generation of those who hate me, but showing love to a thousand generations of those who love me and keep my commandments. (Exodus 20:4-6 NIV)

But what, exactly, does it mean for the Lord to be a "jealous God," or, in another translation, an "impassioned God"? We often think about our passion for the Lord, our jealousy for His kingdom, our zeal for His name and His work. But what about His passion? What about His jealousy for us? His intense yearning for our wellbeing? His zealous love that pursues us and transforms us? Do we understand just how deep and intense that jealous, holy love is?

My good friend Charles Simpson is a man who is zealous for God and passionate about the work of the gospel. In this beautifully written book, he unfolds the meaning of El Kanna, our jealous God, opening the Scriptures with laser focus and sharpening our vision of our impassioned Lord. As you gaze upon Christ, you will be changed!

This book, then, is designed to give you a biblical revelation of the God we serve and love, the God who, in His impassioned love, sent His Son to die for us, the God who, to this very moment, burns with desire to see us know Him and experience Him more deeply. And it is by encountering Him that strongholds are broken in our lives and idols are destroyed!

Are you ready for a fresh encounter with El Kanna? Then keep reading. Your world is about to be rocked.

—**Dr. Michael L. Brown,**
Host of the Line of Fire Broadcast

Introduction

As the pastor of prayer at Times Square Church in the early 1990s, I once preached a sermon on God's jealousy, boldly declaring that idolatry in the life of someone in a covenant relationship with God provokes Him to jealousy! Something happened at that packed altar call that never happened to me before or since. A number of people approached me with their business cards or addresses scribbled on pieces of paper saying, *"If you ever write this in a book, let me know."* That was quite encouraging!

I soon sat down to begin writing my idolatry book, which I never finished until now, over three decades later. Why the delay? A few nights later, our Senior Pastor, David Wilkerson, preached a sermon that was, in my opinion, one of his best ever. The whole church stayed transfixed in their seats in the beautiful Mark Hellenger Theater for over an hour afterwards, softly singing songs of adoration to the Living God who had just spoken loud and clear to us through His servant. At our next weekly staff meeting, I asked Pastor Dave how long it took for him to write such an amazing sermon. With a twinkle in his eyes, he said, "About fifty years!"

He then mentioned that many young ministers asked him to endorse their "books" they wrote and sent to him in manuscript form. Regarding this, he said,

> So many of these young men have not even beg*un* to walk out what they've written about. Just a bunch of lofty, untested ideas. And they have not yet accomplished

anything significant for the Lord. That would be like me writing *The Cross and the Switchblade* before coming to New York City, before confronting Nicky Cruz or starting Teen Challenge! Who would wanna read that?

I had not told Pastor Dave that I was wanting to write a book on God's jealousy because of the response to my recent sermon. So I knew he wasn't speaking directly to me. But God was speaking directly to me *through him*. I sensed the Lord was gently impressing upon me that I needed to live this message out more in my daily walk before writing a book on it. (It's one thing to know the truth, and another thing to live it, and another to live it consistently, and another to live it consistently for a long time!)

With a twinkle in my eyes, I confess to you, dear reader, that this message has taken me well over thirty years to digest, walk out, and then write! By the grace of God, what I will share about God's jealousy has been woven into my relationship with Christ. I'm not just echoing my mentor (David Wilkerson), for I too have gotten to know El Kanna.

Many of us know God as El Shaddai and Jehovah Shalom, and even Jehovah Jireh—that is, we have realized that our God is the Almighty (El Shaddai), that He is our Peace (Jehovah Shalom), and that He is our faithful Provider (Jehovah Jireh). Sometimes such realizations come through face-to-face God-encounters, as with Gideon:

> *Then the Lord turned to him and said, "Peace be with you; do not fear, you shall not die." So Gideon built an altar there to the Lord, and called it The-Lord-Is-Peace [Jehovah Shalom].* (Judges 6:23-24)

But El Kanna, the Jealous God? Is that one of God's hidden names? No, it's not hidden at all. The Lord has declared to us in many places in His Word that He is a jealous God; and even more, that *Jealous is His Name!*

> *You shall worship no other god, for the* Lord, ***whose name is Jealous,*** *is a jealous God.* (Exodus 34:14)

> *You shall have no other gods before Me.... you shall not bow down to them nor serve them.* ***For I, the Lord your God, am a jealous God.*** (Deuteronomy 5:7, 9)

I must adequately give honor to where honor is due. I was so blessed and challenged to sit under the preaching of David Wilkerson for years. Recently, a brother in Christ told me that Pastor Dave's book, *Hungry for More of Jesus,* is his all-time favorite Christian book and he has read it through many times. He almost couldn't believe it when I told him that I literally heard Pastor Dave preach every single chapter from that book as sermons at Times Square Church. Continually hearing such thundering messages about the holiness of God and the Lord's pain over our waywardness prepared me for the life-changing divine encounters I've experienced. (I know the term "life-changing" is overused and often an exaggeration, but looking back now at the fruit those encounters produced, I can confidently say, yes, life-changing.)

I've seen the broken heart of God and I know His jealousy over the idolatry of His people (examining my idolatry first and foremost). But this is not a negative message. It's positive and transformative. **Since God gets overwhelmingly jealous over our misdirected worship, surely He gets overwhelmingly joyful when we get it right and worship Him exclusively.**

And He delights to give us the desire and ability to overcome all idolatry and become as faithful to Him as He is to us, and seeing His jealousy over us is a necessary ingredient.

This book is divided into four parts. Part One examines, through the eyes of five Old Testament prophets, God's jealousy over His chosen nation, Israel. In Chapter One I share how Ezekiel, in the midst of bitter disappointment, received revelation into the personhood of God, realizing how crushed God was over His people's unfaithfulness to Him. In Chapter Two we look at Isaiah's encounter at God's holy throne and how that paralleled my encounter with El Kanna, our Jealous God. In Chapter Three we look at the tragic marriage of Hosea and Gomer, and in Chapter Four we examine the tragic marriage ceremony at Mt. Sinai. In Chapter Five we look at why Jeremiah could not stop weeping over God's wayward people.

In Part Two we examine idolatry, the main cause for divine jealousy. After an overview of Israel's idolatrous history, we look at the idols that have plagued me, the church, and our society. We then see in the post-exile book of Ezra how deeply we are prone towards idolatry, and we see that John the Baptist spoke as a prophet called to expose their root problem, namely, the powerful idol of self.

In Part Three we see the ultimate salvation and deliverance of Israel from all idolatry and how it parallels James' New Testament exhortations, leading us to the freedom found only in a deep, love-relationship with Christ.

Part Four focuses on the glorious, victorious church filled with men and women after God's own heart who exclusively worship and adore our soon-coming Bridegroom-King. When adoration for our God fills our hearts and lives, we will have found the permanent antidote to our constant and intense proneness towards idolatry. What an exciting time to be alive as end-time bridal love will fill, satisfy, and transform those of us who will wholeheartedly adore our soon-coming Groom!

The depths of God's jealousy over us are manifestations of His love, and can motivate us to love Him deeply in return. So may we all come to know El Kanna, The Jealous God through His Word and His Spirit. It's through knowing El Kanna that we are empowered and graced to overcome all idolatry. May what I have experienced, studied, walked out, and written about here assist you in this holy pursuit of discovering the divine jealousy that God has for you, beloved.

HOW HE LOVES

He is jealous for me

Love's like a hurricane, I am a tree

Bending beneath the weight of His wind and mercy

When all of a sudden

I am unaware of these afflictions eclipsed by glory

And I realize just how beautiful You are

And how great Your affections are for me

Oh, how He loves us so

Oh, how He loves us

How He loves us so…

Written by: John Mark McMillan

PART ONE

THE PROPHETS KNEW GOD'S JEALOUSY

CHAPTER 1

Ezekiel: Knowing the Person We've Crushed

"The heavens were opened and I saw visions of God."
—Ezekiel 1:1

Ezekiel had undoubtedly studied and trained for years, eagerly awaiting when he would be able, at the age of thirty, to fulfill his calling as an Old Testament priest in God's temple in Jerusalem. But his life-long dreams would be shattered by the iron fist of the King of Babylon who conquered the sin-filled nation and carried away captives to the land of the Chaldeans. Although Ezekiel's hopes of serving as a priest in the temple were gone, the living God was about to commission him to be a prophet to the people in captivity whose message would touch untold millions in the generations to come, including you and I right now! Our God is a great Compensator! He's able to open the heavens over us no matter what prison shuts us in and even if all our dreams come crashing down! If God allows every door to close around you, He might be getting ready to open a heavenly window over you!

It was in the fires of Babylonian captivity that Judaism was solidified. The children of Israel became acutely aware of the fact that, even though all the outward props of their religion were gone, their God was still with them! They understood deeper than ever before that the God of Israel is the living God over all the Earth and not just another regional deity. Before their captivity was over, even the pagan rulers of Babylon confessed that the God of the Jews (such as Daniel and his three friends) is the one and only Almighty God.[1]

It didn't matter that Ezekiel was a slave in Babylon. God would still use him. He couldn't go into the Holy Place in the temple in Jerusalem where the shekinah glory of God had once dwelt, so the Lord of Glory came to where Ezekiel was. But notice in this deep, dark valley how the Lord revealed Himself to Ezekiel:

> *It came to pass in the thirtieth year...as I was among the captives by the River Chebar, that the heavens were opened, and I saw visions of God...on the likeness of the throne was* ***a likeness with the appearance of a man*** *high above it. This was the appearance of the likeness of the glory of the LORD.* (Ezekiel 1:1, 26)

Although it's easy to become mesmerized with the four dazzling creatures in this first chapter (with their wheels within a wheel), it's what they were carrying that was most important. They were transporting the very throne of God, upon which was the likeness of a man. Why did God reveal

Himself to Ezekiel in this form? He revealed His Personhood to him to imprint upon Ezekiel's heart that God is not an impersonal force, a local deity, or a nebulous spirit; but rather, He is a Person. Our doctrinal statements usually summarize it like this: "The One true God has revealed Himself in three Persons.... as Father, Son, and Holy Spirit."[2] This is not just to be a doctrinal fact stored away in the file cabinets of our minds, but a reality burning in our hearts. Paul wrote,

> *My determined purpose is that I may know Him—that I may progressively become more deeply and intimately acquainted with Him, perceiving and recognizing and understanding the wonders of his person more strongly and more clearly.* (Philippians 3:10, Amplified)

In the midst of Ezekiel's shattered dreams, God came and revealed His Personhood to him. For those of us who have walked with the Lord for any considerable amount of time, we discover that some of our richest experiences come in seasons of anguish. The Lord fulfills His promises to give us *"treasures in the darkness"* and *"streams in the desert."* We find that in our valley experiences that He's there with us, comforting us with His rod and staff, anointing our heads with fresh oil and fresh revelations of Himself. When I experienced the collapse of my "Christian" hopes and dreams, God revealed Himself to me in an amazing way. Let me explain just how devastated I was, and why.

In the Valley of the Shadow of Death

In 1988 the Lord put upon my heart to plant a daughter church to Times Square Church in the South Bronx. I was on staff at Times Square Church, an exciting new work recently started by Bob Phillips, Don Wilkerson, and his brother David Wilkerson, the author of the bestseller, *The Cross and the Switchblade.* After the excitement and glamour of the new church plant wore off, I discovered that full time pastoral ministry is very hard. Pioneering a new church in the South Bronx was not for the faint of heart. And nurturing a flock without the help of a wife was almost impossible.

I had some wonderful experiences the two years I was there. However, towards the end of the second year, I had pushed my body way too hard. I developed a lingering cold, which turned into chronic bronchitis, sinusitis, and then the Epstein Barr virus. My doctor said I was so worn out that I was in danger of getting tuberculosis. I was literally forced to step down because of health problems.

How it broke my heart to resign and hand the work over to Brooklyn Tabernacle, which renamed the church South Bronx Tabernacle. (I'm grateful that Pastor Lugo and his wife took over and faithfully served there for over two decades.) But there was nothing else I could do. I had to step down from this church that I truly poured my heart and soul into. I felt like a total failure, especially since I grew up believing that if I made straight A's in school, then I would be accepted, valued, and loved. It's a difficult thing for someone with that type of upbringing to experience a failure caused by trying too hard to succeed. I knew God Almighty had opened the ministry doors for me in the Bronx, and I felt like it was my lack of wisdom—or my lack of something—that caused me to fail. It's no exaggeration to say that I was totally devastated.

I was walking through a park during this very difficult time in my Christian life when I sensed the Lord leading me to remember what my mother told me many years before. As a frustrated, confused, and hopelessly lost teenager, I felt like it didn't really matter whether I would come home after school or not. "After all," I reasoned within myself, "my parents have eleven other kids. If I run away or get hit by a truck, so what. My absence probably wouldn't even be noticed for days." Thinking my life didn't matter to anyone drove me to the verge of giving in to a life of rebellion that was knocking on my heart's door. Somehow Mom sensed my frustration, and one decisive day she came out to the back porch where I was silently fuming and considering running away, and told me these words:

> Son, I'm sorry that your father works all the time and never takes y'all anywhere. And I'm sorry that I'm so busy that when I do have free time, I'm never able to spend it alone with any of you separately. But I wanna tell you something you must never forget. Regardless of how many children I have, there's a place in my heart that only you can fill. Never forget that.

Those words have stayed with me, for they made a deep impression upon my vulnerable and hurting teenage heart. Being special to someone made all the difference in the world! No longer did I want to rebel. No longer did I feel insignificant. Truly, a turning point in my life.

As I was walking through the park, feeling like a good-for-nothing "Christian" failure, the Lord whispered to my heart, saying,

> Just like your mother told you back then, I, your God tell you now: There's a place *in My heart* that only you can fill. There's a place in Me that only you can reach. For when I created you, I reserved a place in My heart just for

you and you alone, not based upon your achievements, but upon My unfailing love for you.

I can still remember that moment, standing on the green grass as I stood in the presence of the Lord in the park as the sunshine bathed my tear-filled face. My spirit was doing cartwheels inside my broken-down body as I allowed those truths to penetrate. It seemed as though the heavens were opened over my head, and I too saw visions of God.

Yes, God is a Person!

In a deeper way than ever before, I became aware that God is a Person! A Person who has a heart! A Person who has feelings! When I sing to Him from my heart, it actually touches and blesses Him! I received a revelation of God's love towards me that day. It was awesome. Before, I had always equated my worth as a person (even as a believer) by my accomplishments. When I became a seemingly total failure in my own eyes, God came to me in that dark valley and told me how special I was to Him, and not because of what I was doing for Him; just because He loves me and has a special place reserved in His heart for me and me alone. (The same goes for you too, dear reader!) The Lord shared these truths with me during what I thought was total failure on my part because He wanted me to receive and soak in the revelation of His unconditional, individualized love for me which is not based on my accomplishments but on His unfailing love. For a season, the Lord allowed me to feel like a failure so I could experience a new depth of His love for me that reaches far beyond my shortcomings. I received what I would describe as a revelation of the Personhood of God, perhaps a little like Ezekiel experienced long ago by the River Chebar in his land of captivity.

It's one thing to read a verse in the Bible or to hear a sermon preached, and another thing to receive the full impact of what you've heard. That's like the difference between tasting a bite of food and digesting a meal. Ezekiel was told to eat and to digest the message given him before he was to declare it to others:

> *"Son of man... do not be rebellious like that rebellious house; open your mouth and eat what I give you." A roll of a book was therein...So I ate, and it was in my mouth like honey in sweetness.* (Ezekiel 2:8, 3:3)

In the book of Revelation, John had a similar experience:

> *Then I took the little book out of the angel's hand and ate it, and it was as sweet as honey in my mouth. But when I had eaten it (that is, digested it), my stomach became bitter.* (Revelation 10:10)

I believe the revelations given to Ezekiel were also sweet to the taste, at first. But once the truths sank in, they produced what Ezekiel 27:31 describes as *"bitterness of soul, and bitter mourning."* (NASB) What was sweet to Ezekiel at first was the fact that the Person of God was with them in the land of captivity, speaking with him, hurting with him, being with the people of God in their time of sorrow. Similarly, what was sweet to me was the reality that, regardless of whether I succeed or fail in my church planting endeavors, there's still a place in God's heart reserved for me and me alone, for He is a Person. Once this reality was digested into his spirit, Ezekiel painfully realized that the sins that the children of Israel had nonchalantly committed against God deeply wounded Him. Notice what the Lord said through Ezekiel soon afterwards:

> *I will leave a remnant, so that you may have some who escape the sword among the nations... Then those of you who escape will remember Me among the nations where they are carried captive, because* ***I was crushed by their adulterous heart which has departed from Me, and by their eyes which play the harlot after their idols;*** *they will loathe themselves for the evils which they committed in all their abominations.* (Ezekiel 6:8-9)

Wow! The sweet revelations of the Personhood of God to Ezekiel turned into bitterness of soul as he realized how their idolatry had crushed their Lord. Then in Ezekiel Chapter 16, God poignantly describes the early history of Israel as though she were a precious little baby girl. This baby, when she was born, was thrown out into the field to die, depicting her near annihilation in Egypt under the cruel Pharaohs. The Lord comes to this newborn and seeing her in the open field, still stained with the blood of her birth, proclaims one word... "*Live.*" And, of course, she lives... and grows up to become an exceedingly beautiful young woman. The Lord then enters a marriage covenant with her and floods her with gifts and she becomes a splendid Queen. This woman's response to this kindness is to enter into an unbelievably immoral lifestyle.

> *You trusted in your own beauty, played the harlot because of your fame, and poured out your harlotry on everyone passing by who would have it. Moreover, you multiplied your acts of harlotry as far as the land of the trader, Chaldea; and even then, you were not satisfied. How degenerate is your heart! says the* Lord *GOD, seeing you do all these things, the deeds of a brazen harlot. You are an adulterous wife, who takes strangers instead of her husband.*
>
> (Ezekiel 16:15, 29, 30)

If you were the husband to this type of woman, your heart would be crushed and filled with jealousy.

Crushed By Our Unfaithfulness

Yes, God is a Person, a Person crushed by our unfaithfulness to Him. I began to let Ezekiel's view of God in Chapter Six, Verse nine sink into my heart, reading these verses in other translations:

> **New Living Translation:** They will recognize how hurt I am by their unfaithful hearts and lustful eyes that long for their idols.
>
> **Complete Jewish Bible:** How broken I have been over their whoring hearts that left me, and over their eyes that went whoring after their idols!
>
> **Amplified Bible:** Those of you who escape will remember Me among the nations to which they will be exiled, how I have been broken by their lewdness and their adulterous hearts which have turned away from Me, and by their eyes which lust after their idols.

CHAPTER 2

Isaiah: Seeing the Lightning-Like, Radiant King

"I saw the Lord sitting on a throne, high and lifted up."
—Isaiah 6:1

I could tell it was going to be a refreshingly warm and sunny spring day. I was wishing I didn't have to officiate a funeral, and yet I was willing to help the grieving family find God's comfort in their time of need. These were the thoughts that were occupying my mind as I took my black suit jacket out of the hallway closet and slipped it on. "Oh, good," I thought to myself as I looked over the front of the suit, "it's clean." I straightened my tie, combed my hair one last time, and headed out the door of our Queens apartment while making sure our kitty didn't sneak out with me.

After closing the front door of the building, I turned around on its small porch and faced the bright sun that was beaming down as though it was just a few hundred yards away. I paused to catch my breath and enjoy the springtime warmth that was a long time in coming after a harsh New York City winter. My enjoyment of the moment vanished as I looked down at my black suit. Cat hairs were everywhere! What appeared clean in normal lighting was filthy in the bright sunlight. It took at least ten minutes to wipe all the hairs off and remove the smudges (that I could see). Afterwards, I jogged to my car, determined to still make it to the funeral home in time. It wouldn't be until sometime later when reading through the book of Isaiah that I realized the spiritual lessons contained in my black suit incident. The parallels are many and the lessons are powerful.

Talk about a life-changing encounter with God! When Isaiah *"saw the Lord sitting on a throne, high and lifted up"* it absolutely floored him. Standing in the presence of a holy God as the glory of the Lord shone upon him, he looked at the "suit" of his life and immediately became aware of uncleanness that, prior to this, was either undetected or seemingly insignificant to him. Remember, we're talking about an Old Testament prophet whom the Scriptures say was one of the *"holy men of God who spoke as they were moved upon by the Holy Spirit."* (2 Peter 1:21) Isaiah seems to have already been ministering the Word of the Lord for five chapters prior to this encounter in Chapter Six. Even so, seeing God made him aware of the uncleanness of his speech.

Since Isaiah grew up in a society that was characterized by unclean speaking, (Isaiah 6:5) he must have excused his gossiping, his coarse jesting, or his loose tongue as merely a cultural character trait. Perhaps after religious services, Isaiah and his prophet buddies would get a bite to eat in a nearby kosher diner where they would eat roast lamb and discuss the latest news coming down the prophetic grapevine: "Did you hear about what Hosea's planning? He's considering marrying that woman, Gomer. What a mistake that would be! Mark my words: That marriage won't last six months." Or "Can you believe what Ezekiel said the other day; that the Holy Spirit actually lifted him up and carried him away by a lock of his hair! (Ezekiel 8:3) The Holy Spirit doesn't do stuff like that. That's not of God. Ezekiel always was a little weird, you know."

And then Isaiah suffered a major tragedy. King Uzziah died, and Isaiah was hurting for two reasons: Judah lost a godly king (which was rare commodity in those days), and Isaiah personally suffered the loss of his friend, Uzziah. This season of mourning probably caused the prophet to go to the temple even more than ever to pray and seek God and pour out his grieving soul. During perhaps one of those quiet times, the Almighty God suddenly appears in His temple. Upon seeing His glory, Isaiah was instantly aware of his uncleanness and cries out,

> *Woe is me, for I am undone! Because I am a man of unclean lips, and I dwell in the midst of a people of unclean lips; for my eyes have seen the King, the Lord of Hosts.*
>
> (Isaiah 6:5)

Heaven responds to that desperate cry in an amazing way as one of the seraphim came,

> *...having in his hand a live coal which he had taken with the tongs from the altar. And he touched my mouth with it,*

and said: "Behold, this has touched your lips; your iniquity is taken away, and your sin purged." (Isaiah 6:6)

After working for the Lord in New York City for many years, I was blessed with an all-expense-paid vacation to beautiful San Diego. My friends Wally, Don Meggelin, and I spent the morning in the home of our friends, Mary Ann Peluso and her mom, Victoria. As we started planning the day in front of us, there was a difference of opinion as to what we should do. Our host and her mom wanted to take us to one of the finest restaurants in the area, located right on the awesome La Jolla shore. Wally and Don, however, were determined to drive down to Mexico to minister to the desperately poor who live in the nearby border towns.

As for me, I woke up that morning feeling so un-oppressed and so refreshed, and so close to the Lord that I just wanted to spend time with Him. Finally, the two groups stood up and decided to split up and do what each one wanted. As Mary Ann was getting her keys out of her purse to lock the front door on her way out, she looked over at me, still sitting on the couch.

Not wanting to seem overly spiritual, I whispered to her, "Would you mind.... if I just stayed here today.... and prayed?"

"No problem," she graciously smiled and replied. "If you want, help yourself to the leftovers in the refrigerator. We'll see you this afternoon." With that, she gently closed the door behind her.

Ah, quiet! I did not want to minister to the poor, and I did not want to eat any more. I recently had plenty of both in New York City. I just wanted to spend uninterrupted, unscheduled, unpressured time with Jesus, who lately had been pushed out of my hectic life of crisis-filled, urban pastoring.

I looked up past the sparkling living room light and said, “Lord, Jesus, I just wanna be with You today!” As those sincere words came out of my lips, I somehow sensed they really touched His heart. Tears freely flowed down my face as I got on my knees to pray to the One whom I realize deeper than ever is a Person, Someone who is touched with the feelings of our infirmities. (Hebrews 4:16)

As I reached out to the Lord with a fresh desire to really know Him, He graciously drew near. His presence electrified, permeated, and filled the living room. I became, not only aware, but also immersed in His holiness and spotless purity in a way I had never even remotely experienced before. He allowed me to see (not with my natural eyes, but with the eyes of my heart) a small glimpse of His overwhelming, radiant glory. What really overshadowed every thought and feeling racing through my being was the reality of the whiteness, the brightness, the purity of Him. It reminded me of a wedding dress whose color represents moral faithfulness. I could actually “feel” the purity of His faithfulness towards me. I somehow knew what He was going to say to me even before I heard Him.

And then He spoke. Not an audible voice, yet it was that unmistakable, still small voice of my Shepherd. (John 10:27) He spoke to me as though I was His mate, as though we were married, as though He was a wounded spouse! His words pierced through my very being:

> Since the day that we have come into a covenant relationship with each other, I have been totally loyal and completely faithful to you, just as I promised. You,

however, have not lived up to your commitment to Me. Over and over you have wavered in your faithfulness and love towards Me.

I saw the Lord (with the eyes of my heart) and I heard Him (with the ears of my spirit); and in so doing, I really saw myself and my shortcomings. In the Light that exposes all darkness, I realized that although I also promised my love and loyalty to Christ, I had not been living up to those promises. Repeatedly I've given my heart to other things and other people. I've forgotten, neglected, and unappreciated Jesus Christ and His love for me, and this pierces His heart with the pain of a betrayed spouse.

Wow! I somehow knew the Lord was not going to give Himself in a deeper way to me...until I faced the fact of how much my spiritually adulterous ways have crushed Him.

A Life-Changing Encounter

From that day forward, I have been a different person. At that holy moment, I wasn't aware that this was the beginning of God answering years of praying for a deeper relationship with Jesus. I just felt unclean, unfaithful, defiled—a spiritual adulterer. Up to that point, I had always looked lightly at the many times my heart was wrapped up in other things (even godly, God-given, and God-appointed things), instead of being wrapped up in the Person of Jesus Christ. I used to rationalize my actions by saying, "Aren't we all like that, at times?" or "But I'm more on fire than a lot of Christians I know." Yet, my Lord was allowing me to see that I had put my heart on many other things besides Him, the One to whom my heart's affections are due.

"But, Lord," I used to reason, "doesn't everyone from time-to-time drift away from total devotion to You? I've served You all these years without ever going back into the world. Most people who know me would say that I've been on fire for God ever since I was saved. I work very hard for You in New York City, and I'm totally committed to the advancement of Your kingdom and doing whatever You want me to do." But the One who knows me better than I know myself was revealing truth to me and bringing to my recollection the times my heart became cold toward Him and captivated by other things and other people to the point of neglecting and ignoring Him, provoking Him to jealousy.

While I knelt in His presence that day, crying and contemplating His words and literally soaking in the reality of His utter faithfulness to me, I didn't feel condemned. Unclean? Yes. Undone? Absolutely. But not condemned. I somehow and immediately knew this encounter would correct and change me, and that's a good thing. I found myself declaring from the depths of my being words like Isaiah's:

> Woe is me, for I am undone. For I am a man of wavering faithfulness and I dwell in the midst of a church of wavering faithfulness. I am suddenly and extremely aware of this because I have been granted a glimpse of the unwavering faithfulness of my Lord.

Just as the clean, white wedding gown upon the Bride of Christ in the Book of Revelation represents moral uprightness, I knew the lightning-like radiance of Jesus' clothing represented His spousal moral perfection… towards me. Revelation 19:8 in the Amplified Bible says,

> She has been permitted to dress in fine linen, dazzling white and clean—for the fine linen signifies the righteous acts of the saints [the ethical conduct, personal integrity, moral courage, and godly character of believers].

Regarding Jesus, we read:

> *He was transfigured before them. His face shone like the sun, and His clothes became* ***as white as the light.*** *(Matthew 17:2)* ***His clothes became shining, exceedingly white, like snow,*** *such as no launderer on earth can whiten them.* (Mark 9:3)

I knew God would not send an angel with a hot coal to instantly burn the exposed iniquity out of me. This wasn't simply an unclean lips (or speech) problem like Isaiah's, but rather, a deeper heart issue. Instead of sending a purging, fiery coal, Jesus planted something in me that day as small as a mustard seed. But if nurtured and cared for properly, I knew it would grow into the largest tree in the garden of my heart. This mustard seed I'll describe as a God-given desire to become a man after God's own heart. More than a successful ministry, more than spiritual power and authority, I desire above all else to be a person who worships God alone, a man who truly and faithfully runs after the heart of God. "Lord, give me that heart, a heart that is completely idol-free."

His manifest presence remained with me in that living room in San Diego all day long. When the hosts and other guests returned that evening, they all spoke in whispered tones for the first half hour as they too sensed Him in our midst in an awesome way. Weeks later, although my spirit knew I had experienced a life-altering encounter with the Lord, my mind began to question the validity of it all. Would God really relate to me like a wounded spouse? Would He "feel" that way about me? Is He really jealous over the people and things that I have made more important than Him? Do the Scriptures line up with what I've experienced? Now that this encounter is years behind me, I can literally see the good fruit it has produced. A genuine, divine encounter; one that you don't speak about too often or too soon, lest you water down something extremely special.

Three Vital Questions

I needed to see that the direction I was being led into was firmly grounded in the Scriptures. Three specific questions arose in my heart that I brought to my personal Bible study over the next few months:

1. Would God relate to us like a wounded spouse?
2. Is this view of God (having such deep feelings and emotions) even scriptural?
3. But isn't jealousy sinful? How can God possibly be jealous?

Before I could comfortably continue down this trail, I needed to have my Shepherd lead me into the green pastures of His Word to find answers to those three important questions. I soon found myself studying the book of Hosea the prophet, the brokenhearted spouse who wrote about another brokenhearted Spouse.

CHAPTER 3

Hosea: Feeling What a Brokenhearted Husband Feels

"Love a woman, beloved… yet an adulteress."
—Hosea 3:2, KJV

In the prophetic book of Hosea—one of those minor prophets with a major message—God gave a graphic illustration of Israel's spiritual condition by having a prophet marry a woman whom God foresaw would eventually turn to prostitution. (Some say Hosea married a prostitute, but with their future children being spoken of in the present, Gomer's prostitution may have also been in the future, although spoken of as if also being in the present). The Lord said to Hosea:

> *Go, take yourself a wife of harlotry and children of harlotry, for the land has committed great harlotry by departing from the LORD.* (Hosea 1:3)

I can imagine Hosea saying to himself, "God will use me to help Gomer grow in the Lord. He must know her heart." God surely did know her heart, and her unfaithful heart towards Hosea broke his heart to an unimaginable degree. Then he knew from experience just how God felt towards unfaithful Israel. I imagine God telling him, "Now that you know how I'm feeling, you can speak to adulterous Israel on My behalf." Or perhaps, even more accurately, "Now that you've gone through what I've been going through, you can love your wife like I love My wayward people."

> *The LORD said to me, "Go again, love a woman who is loved by a lover and is committing adultery, just like the love of the LORD for the children of Israel, who look to other gods..."* (Hosea 3:1)

Throughout this book, we can sense the hurt and jealousy and righteous anger of God. This prophecy was God's final attempt to call Israel to repentance before having to release her to overdue chastisement. We see God's intense love for His people and His desire to redeem them from their iniquities. The infidelity of Hosea's wife is a graphic illustration of Israel's (and our) unfaithfulness. Gomer runs after other men. Israel runs after other gods. We run after so many other things. Gomer commits physical adultery, while Israel is committing spiritual adultery.

Here in Hosea, we find the reaction of a spouse who withdraws their love...until the guilty party faces up to their sins and realizes how deeply their selfish actions have hurt their mate.

> *With their flocks and herds, they shall go to seek the LORD, but they will not find Him; He has withdrawn Himself*

> *from them (because)…they have dealt treacherously with the LORD. I will go away…till they acknowledge their offense. Then they will seek My face; in their affliction they will earnestly seek Me.* (5:6, 7, 14, 15)

The first three chapters of Hosea summarize his tragic marriage and in the remaining nine chapters God deals with His disastrous relationship with His people. Before Hosea's prophetic message begins, we are given a glimpse of the love of God revealed through Hosea as he brought his wayward wife back home and pleaded with her to cease from her adulterous ways.

> *I said to her, "You shall stay with me many days; you shall not play the harlot, nor shall you have a man—so, too, will I be toward you."* (Hosea 3:3)

In Chapter Nine we read, *"Do not rejoice, O Israel, with joy like other peoples, for you have played the harlot against your God."* (9:1) The Lord describes the anguish of having to judge the unfaithful nation:

> *How can I give you up, Ephraim? How can I hand you over, Israel? My heart churns within Me; My sympathy is stirred. I will not execute the fierceness of My anger; I will not again destroy Ephraim. For I am God, and not man.* (Hosea 11:8-9)

Although God in His love would hold back the fierceness of His righteous anger, Israel could not go utterly unpunished because their sinfulness kept increasing:

> *Now they sin more and more, and have made for themselves molded images, idols of their silver, according to their skill; all of it is the work of craftsmen.* (Hosea 13:2)

God's Emotional Response to Our Sins

This view of God's anger and pain is often overlooked in our selfish society and our self-centered type of American Christianity. However, you don't have to read very far into God's revelation of Himself to mankind before you begin to see His deep, emotional reactions to our sins. In Genesis we read:

> *The Lord saw that the wickedness of man was great in the earth, and that every imagination of the thoughts of his heart was only evil continually. And the Lord was sorry that He had made man on the earth, and* ***it grieved Him to His heart.*** (Genesis 6:5-6)

A few thousand years later, we hear of God's anguish over Israel's unfaithfulness to Him.

> *How often they rebelled against Him in the wilderness, and* ***grieved Him*** *in the desert! Again and again they tempted God,* ***and pained the Holy One of Israel.*** (Psalm 78:40-41 NASB)

"Grieved" in Hebrew means to hurt, to grieve, and to cause pain; and "pained" literally means to scrape to pieces. Paul in the New Testament uses the same word grieve in the book of Ephesians. *"Do not grieve the Holy Spirit of God."* (4:29) God's reaction to our sinning against Him hasn't changed. Old Testament scholar Terence Fretheim comments,

> God is revealed not as one who remains coolly unaffected by the rejection of the people, but as one who is deeply wounded by the broken relationship. The interaction between God and people [as seen in the Old Testament] thus takes place not simply at the intellectual level…or

> in a law court…[but] also at the emotional level. God shares feelings, not just thoughts. The people know not only what God thinks, but what God feels.[3]

One of my favorite Scriptures in the Bible is an obscure verse in Isaiah concerning God's heart towards His people: *"In all their affliction He was afflicted…"* (63:9) In the book of Judges we read this about God: *"His soul could no longer endure the misery of Israel."* (Judges 10:16) Surely, the greatest revelation of the heart of God is seen when we recognize that *"The Word became flesh and dwelt among us."* (John 1:14) Jesus Christ is the express image of the Father or as the Amplified says is *"the perfect imprint and very image of God's nature."* (Hebrews 1:3) Isaiah informs us that He was *"a man of sorrows and acquainted with grief."* (53:3) Jesus wept over the people of Jerusalem who rejected the salvation He came to give them. (Matthew 23:37) He wept at Lazarus's tomb, partly because He was sharing in the grief Mary and Martha were experiencing. He is the great High Priest who is *"touched with the feeling of our infirmities."* (Hebrews 4:15)

God experiences a whole range of intense emotions in His relationship with us. In Zephaniah He is seen greatly rejoicing and singing over His people:

> *The* LORD *your God in your midst, the Mighty One, will save; He will rejoice over you with gladness, He will quiet you with His love, He will rejoice over you with singing.*
> (Zephaniah 3:17)

"Rejoice" here in Hebrew refers to spinning around under the influence of any violent emotion, such as joy. The Lord rejoices over us and delights in us, taking great pleasure in us. What an incredible God we have: a Person Who can be blessed, be delighted by, and be joyful in His people; or Who can be grieved, wounded, and hurt to a depth we could never imagine and, for the most part, have hardly even begun to realize.

Is This the God of the Bible?

And yet, I wondered.... joy and grief in the heart of God depending on *my* responses? Is that even scriptural? Is that the God of the Bible? Doesn't God declare in Psalm 50:12, *"If I were hungry, I would not tell you; for the world is Mine, and all its fullness."* And Paul said in Acts 17:24-25,

> God, who made the world and everything in it, since He is Lord of heaven and earth, does not dwell in temples made with hands. Nor is He worshiped with men's hands, ***as though He needed anything,*** since He gives to all life, breath, and all things.

God is so immense and holy and perfect that He doesn't need anything and surely not anything I can give in order for Him to be happy. Right? Perhaps a better way to describe seeing God's heart for us is that we behold His emotions. Our self-centered society isn't conducive for developing people who are concerned about how God feels. But it's not just our society that we must blame for this. When the early Church leaders tried to doctrinally preserve the truths of Scripture, sometimes they swung the pendulum too far the other way. For example, at the Council of Chalcedon (A.D. 451) they condemned... *"those who dare to say that the Godhead of the Only Begotten is capable of suffering."*[4] The Westminster Confession of Faith (A.D. 1646) says,

> There is but one only, living, and true God, who is infinite in being and perfection, a most pure spirit, invisible, without body, parts, or passions, immutable… [5]

Why would church leaders teach that God is without passion and incapable of suffering? The church has historically affirmed the doctrine of the impassibility of God because since He is immutable (unchanging), He therefore must be impassible (incapable of suffering). The dictionary describes impassible as, "not subject to suffering, pain, or harm; unfeeling; impassive." In the article, *The Emotions of Jesus*, New Testament professor G. Walter Hansen writes,

> Many theologians throughout history have argued strongly that God is not moved by emotions. This doctrine of the impassibility of God, developed by early Christian apologists such as Justin Martyr, sought to distinguish the God of the Bible from pagan gods whose passions led them into all kinds of scandalous behavior. What they meant to emphasize was that God does not have mad, shameful passions like the gods of pagan mythology.[6]

Professor Dennis Ngien wrote,

Virtually all the early church fathers took it [divine impassibility] for granted, denying God any emotions because they might interrupt His tranquility.[7]

As we have discussed earlier, you cannot read the Bible very long without seeing the emotions of God. And Christ, who came to reveal the Father's heart to us, was motivated by compassion (Matthew 9:36), expressed His anger (Mark 3:5), suffered agonizing grief (Luke 22:44), and experienced deep joy (Luke 10:21). Marcel Sarot observed,

> The number of adherents to the doctrine of divine impassibility has continuously decreased during the present century. Slowly but surely the concept of an immutable and impassible God has given way to the concept of a sensitive, emotional, passionate God.[8]

> Theologian Ronald Goetz writes, "The age-old dogma that God is impassible and immutable, incapable of suffering, is for many no longer tenable. The… (teaching) that God suffers has, in fact, become the new orthodoxy."[9]

The first two of my three questions were sufficiently answered. Yes, the Bible shows a hurting God withdrawing from His people like a betrayed spouse until they acknowledge their sins; and yes, the Bible's view is that of a very emotional God. But isn't jealousy a sinful emotion? To adequately answer my third question, let's look at the greatest prophet in the Old Testament, namely Moses.

CHAPTER 4

Moses: Understanding an "Over the Top" Jealous Husband

"I, the LORD your God, am a jealous God."
—Exodus 20:5

The first image that comes to my mind when the name Moses is mentioned is usually that of an angry old man with stone tablets raised over his head—frozen in time; right before those ignored Ten Commandment tablets are violently thrown to the ground. Religiously terrifying. It is true that God was very angry with Israel, and Moses was extremely mad at his brother. Aaron, who was put in charge of the camp while Moses was communing with God on the mountaintop, had an amazing but false explanation as to how his golden calf came into existence:

> *Moses said to Aaron, "What did this people do to you that you have brought so great a sin upon them?" So Aaron said, "Do not let the anger of my lord become hot. You know the people, that they are set on evil. For they said to me, 'Make us gods that shall go before us; as for this Moses, the man who brought us out of the land of Egypt, we do not know what has become of him.' And I said to them, 'Whoever has any gold, let them break it off.' So they gave it to me, and I cast it into the fire, and this calf came out.'"*
> (Exodus 32:24)

I can see why Moses was angry with lying Aaron. But perhaps Aaron and the people didn't know any better. After all, they left Egypt only a few weeks before this. Maybe all they knew was Egyptian calf worship? Not according to Scripture. Long before this famous golden calf incident, God spoke to them specifically about staying away from the abominable idols in Egypt. They had already rebelled to the point that He rebuked them even before they left Egypt! Here's what Ezekiel adds to the story:

> *On the day when I chose Israel… and made Myself known to them in the land of Egypt… I said, "Each of you, throw away the abominations which are before his eyes, and do not defile yourselves with the idols of Egypt." They rebelled against Me and would not obey Me…nor did they forsake the idols of Egypt. Then I said, "I will pour out My fury on them and fulfill My anger against them in the midst of the land of Egypt." But I acted for My name's sake, that it should not be profaned before the Gentiles.* (20:5-10)

Moses (and the Lord through Moses) appeared to be extremely jealous of this golden calf worship. Why was the

Lord so very angry with Israel's misplaced worship? And why is God's jealousy here "over the top," causing Him to be described as a consuming fire?

> *Take heed to yourselves, lest you forget the covenant of the* L*ORD your God which He made with you, and make for yourselves a carved image in the form of anything which the* L*ORD your God has forbidden you. For the* L*ORD your God is a consuming fire, a jealous God.* (Deuteronomy 4:23-24)

Why was God so jealous? The answer can be found by going back to the very beginning, the book of Genesis. When Moses wrote Genesis—under divine inspiration and direction—he started with the creation of the heavens and the earth and then moved to the creation of the first marriage. After Adam's wonder-filled heart exclaimed his appreciation and love for his newly created spouse next to him, Moses then added an interesting footnote, a commentary to Adam's exclamation:

> Adam said: "*This is now bone of my bones and flesh of my flesh; she shall be called Woman, because she was taken out of Man.*" (Genesis 2:23)

> Moses then commented: "*Therefore a man shall leave his father and mother and be joined to his wife, and they shall become one flesh.*" (Genesis 2:24)

Adam did not have to leave a father and mother to be joined to Eve! So Moses was commenting on the characteristics of the institute of future marriages. Since Eve was bone of his bone and flesh of his flesh, Moses comments that this "joining" of the Man and Woman shall be very special, marked by deep unity and a complete prioritizing over all other relationships; an exclusivity all its own. Raymond Ortlund writes about the Hebrew word for joining (or, cleaving, in the KJV):

> The word רכק to the Hebrews means not simply to cleave but lovingly and with marital fondness…marital love with which a husband should care for, cherish, and nourish his wife as his own bone and flesh.[10]

God (through Moses' writings) in the very beginning defined marriage as an exclusive, prioritized, loving relationship between a husband and wife. And this covenant that God and Israel entered at Sinai was a marriage covenant. Again, Ezekiel adds more clarity to the narrative:

> *I swore a solemn oath to you [at Mt. Sinai] and entered into a marriage covenant with you, declares the Sovereign* L*ORD*, *and you became mine.* (Ezekiel 16:8 NET)

> *My covenant…they broke, though I was a husband to them, says the* L*ORD.* (Jeremiah 31:3)

Hosea's wife, after they had been married long enough to have three children, afterwards went into a life of prostitution, becoming extremely unfaithful to her husband and breaking their marriage vows of exclusivity. But with Moses, before the honeymoon was even over, Israel prostituted herself with the golden calf; the equivalent of a bride having sex with the best man while the reception was still going on! In doing so, they broke the covenant they had just made with their God. Moses remembered the episode as he wrote the book of Deuteronomy:

> *The LORD our God made a covenant with us...saying, "I am the LORD your God who brought you out of the land of Egypt, out of the house of bondage. You shall have no other gods before Me...you shall not bow down to them nor serve them. For I, the LORD your God, am a jealous God."* (Deuteronomy 5:2, 8, 9)

The Lord then gave them the rest of the Ten Commandments, the basis of the agreement (or covenant) between God and the nation of Israel. God promised to be their Provider, Protector, Helper, and Husband. They in turn, vowed to be His people, obeying Him and worshipping Him alone. In Exodus 24:3 this nation-bride collectively answers with an "I do" like a bride agreeing to fulfil her wedding vows.

> *Moses came and told the people all the words of the LORD and all the judgments. And all the people answered with one voice and said, "All the words which the LORD has said we will do."*

This covenant is often summarized in these words: *"I will be your God, and you shall be My people."* (Exodus 6:7; Leviticus 26:12; Jeremiah 7:23; Ezekiel 36:28) In other words, God Himself vowed, "I will be exclusively yours, and you will be exclusively Mine."

Yes, the nation of Israel breaking this covenant right after making it would be like a wife being unfaithful to her husband right after they got married. No wonder God was provoked to such intense jealousy! The Psalmist wrote, *"They provoked Him to anger with their high places and moved Him to jealousy with their carved images."* (Psalm 78:58) The Lord said through Ezekiel, *"I will judge you as women who break wedlock or shed blood are judged; I will bring blood upon you in fury and jealousy."* (16:38)

The Lord's Overlooked Name: El Kanna

Everything about God is perfect, even His jealousy over us which is certainly not based on any insecurity on His part. Rather, it stems from His longing for intimacy with us which He knows is the only thing that will truly satisfy our needy souls. Even so, how is it that the Lord can be described as a jealous God? How can jealousy be in His holy heart? Isn't it a sinful and selfish trait? Jealous is not only an adjective describing the Lord, but it's also one of His self-revealing names. For instance, we know that Jehovah Jireh is "the Lord who will provide," Jehovah Rapha is "the Lord our Healer," and El Shaddai is "the Almighty God." But what about El Kanna, the Lord's overlooked Name? That's translated in most English versions as "the Lord whose Name is Jealous."

Since this word is used almost exclusively in our English language today to describe something negative, it does seem strange at first to think of God as being even slightly *jealous.* After all, Solomon wrote, *"Jealousy arouses a husband's fury,"* (Proverbs 6:34) and Paul labeled it as one of the acts of our fallen, sinful nature; one of the works of the flesh. (Galatians 5:19) When I think of jealousy, I picture a boyfriend becoming enraged at a rival's attempts to take his place, or of a wife who's overly possessive of her husband, perhaps exposing insecurities in her (although sometimes jealousy is fully warranted).

The Hebrew word for jealousy is from a root word that literally means, "to become dark red." As with other emotions such as anger, jealousy can be either morally good or bad, depending on its object. If the object is self, the results are hatred, envy, and strife. However, the Bible speaks also of a divine jealousy, a consuming single-minded pursuit of good not rooted in selfishness, but rooted in the welfare of another. When Paul speaks about the jealousy he had for his beloved Christian brothers and sisters in Corinth, he described it as a godly jealousy.

> *I am jealous for you with a godly jealousy; for I betrothed you to one husband, to present you as a pure virgin to Christ. But I am afraid that, as the serpent deceived Eve by his trickery, your minds will be led astray from sincere and pure devotion to Christ.* (2 Corinthians 11:2, 3 NASB)

It goes without saying that the jealousy of our holy God is also godly. Everything about Him is surely godly! So, when God's covenant people indulge in idolatry, it is spiritual adultery that provokes His jealousy. We may think God is a passive observer of our unfaithfulness, but that would be as ungodly as the husband Raymond Ortlund describes:

> What sort of husband would look at his wayward wife and dismiss her adulteries by mumbling, "As long as she and her lovers don't shake the bed and make too much noise, as long as I can get my sleep, what's the big deal? It's only marriage!"? No one but a knave [an evil, unprincipled person] would own such a sentiment. So how can we trivialize our covenant with God? The covenant is a marriage. It is *the* marriage.[11]

Paul Copan adds,

> A wife who doesn't get jealous and angry when another woman is flirting with her husband isn't really all that committed to the marriage relationship. A marriage

> without the potential for jealousy when an intruder threatens isn't much of a marriage. Outrage, pain, anguish—these are the appropriate responses to such a deep violation.[12]

Coming to grips with God's holy, fervent jealousy over us causes us to remain on the operating table when the Spirit of God seeks to probe our hearts for the disease of spiritual unfaithfulness. It's truly a spiritual cancer, and if left untreated, will wreak havoc in our souls. God hates idolatry because He has made Himself an absolute enemy to anything and everything that will bring harm to us, His beloved people. Having seeds of idolatry sprouting in the soil of our hearts is so serious that He urgently calls us to repentance whenever He sees that we are going (or have gone) off track—like in the days of Jeremiah, the weeping prophet.

CHAPTER 5

Jeremiah: Hearing a Husband Who Couldn't Stop Weeping

"My people have forgotten Me, days without number."
—Jeremiah 2:32

The Lord wept and spoke through Jeremiah as they suffered the pain caused by the adulteries of God's people. Commenting on Jeremiah 2:32, David Wilkerson wrote,

> He has said openly, *"My people neglect Me for days on end!"* Every generation has read about it. Yet, why would the Lord tell the whole world about such neglect? Shouldn't lovers' differences be kept quiet? No—He wants us to know how hurt He is! He tells the whole world because He is so heartbroken by our behavior! Jeremiah was weeping with holy tears that weren't his

own. Indeed, this prophet heard God speak of His own weeping, broken heart.[13]

Pastor Dave's words carry much weight with me partly because I saw him often weep for God's wayward church, both publicly and privately.

Throughout this prophetic book it's hard to distinguish when God is doing the weeping and when it's Jeremiah. That's because God wept through him, and Jeremiah wept for God. Like Christ, Jeremiah wept over the people as he saw them heading toward destruction. We have preachers like Jonah who declare God's Word, but don't carry within them God's heart. Jonah was angry when God spared the people of Nineveh. They were Israel's political enemy and Jonah was more patriotic than godly, more into politics than evangelism. In Jonah, Chapter 3 we read of the repentance of Nineveh followed by the mercy of God and the disappointment of Jonah.

> *Then God saw their works, that they turned from their evil way; and God relented from the disaster that He had said He would bring upon them, and He did not do it. But it displeased Jonah exceedingly, and he became angry. So he prayed to the LORD, and said, "Ah, Lord, was not this what I said when I was still in my country? Therefore I fled previously to Tarshish; for I know that You are a gracious and merciful God, slow to anger and abundant in lovingkindness, One who relents from doing harm."*
> (Jonah 3:10, 4:1)

It's obvious, that although Jonah had the Word of the Lord for Nineveh, he did not have the heart of God for them. His initial reluctance to go was because he knew the message of judgment from a merciful God could bring repentance and the revoking of judgment. God, who delights in mercy, sometimes raises up strong prophetic warnings in order to avoid calamity. God not only told Jeremiah what to preach, but also told him what the purpose was for such a hard message:

> *Then the word of the LORD came to me, saying: "The instant I speak concerning a nation and concerning a kingdom, to pluck up, to pull down, and to destroy it, if that nation against whom I have spoken turns from its evil, I will relent of the disaster that I thought to bring upon it."* (18:5, 7-8)

Can you imagine being married to a wife whom you think loves you as much as you love her, which is with all your heart. But one day you unexpectedly come home early from work and catch her in bed with another man! How would you feel? But what if she assured you that it was a moral slip in a moment of weakness and it would never, ever happen again. What if a week later you decide to come home early with a bouquet of flowers to surprise and bless her, and you find her in bed with a different man than the first one! Then you find out that she's slept with several men in the neighborhood! How would you feel? The angry and jealous feelings you would have if you could express them into words would be the message God spoke to adulterous Israel through Jeremiah, the prophet who could not stop weeping. His prophecies have one main theme—Israel, like an unfaithful wife, has committed spiritual adultery over and over against her Lord. Listen to Jeremiah's first sermon which sets the tone for the whole book:

> *The word of the LORD came to me, saying, "Go and cry in the hearing of Jerusalem, saying, 'Thus says the LORD: I remember you, the kindness of your youth,* ***the love of your betrothal, when you went after Me in the wilderness...***

> *Israel was holiness to the* Lord*. What injustice have your fathers found in Me, that they have gone far from Me, and have followed idols?'"* (Jeremiah 2:1-5)

This is a picture of a slighted husband, painfully remembering how much his unfaithful wife once loved him. Another version reads:

> *"I remember the devotion of your youth,* **how as a bride you loved me...**" *(NIV)* The Amplified Bible says: *"I earnestly remember the kindness and devotion of your youth, your love after your betrothal in Egypt and marriage at Sinai."*

> David Wilkerson wrote: Jesus knows what it is like to be cheated on! He has been patient and longsuffering as all through history His beloved Israel has been unfaithful to Him, committing spiritual adultery over and over again.[14]

The Lord tried to show His people the wickedness of their spiritual adulteries through Jeremiah:

> *Has a nation changed its gods, which are not gods? But My people have changed their Glory for what does not profit. My people have committed two evils: They have forsaken Me, the fountain of living waters, and hewn themselves cisterns—broken cisterns that can hold no water... You said, "I will not transgress," when* ***on every high hill and under every green tree you lay down, playing the harlot.*** (Jeremiah 2:11-13, 20)

> Dr. Michael Brown, in his Commentary on Jeremiah, wrote, "God promises to 'scatter' her, which is her rightful lot and portion, measured out by Yahweh himself as the

> consequence for her idolatry, the sin that always lies at the root of her punishment, being **the sin that most directly offends the Lord. It is abandonment. It is ingratitude. It is adultery. It is betrayal.** It is the ultimate insult, the height of spiritual insanity, to turn away from the eternal God and bow down to sticks and stones."[15]

> The third chapter of Jeremiah begins with another fiery rebuke. The Amplified Bible says, Lift up your eyes to the bare heights and see; **where have you not been adulterously lain with?** (In other words, you've committed adultery so many times it's hard to find a place where you haven't.) By the waysides you have sat waiting for lovers eager for idolatry. And you have polluted the land with your vile harlotry and your wickedness, unfaithfulness and disobedience to God.

Jeremiah the weeping prophet lamented over the horrible destruction of Jerusalem which he witnessed firsthand and wrote about in his second book called Lamentations. God wept through him as He observed the cause of such destruction, the adulteries of His bride, Israel.

Dr. Brown wrote:

> The prophet had a deep, personal relationship with God, sharing the Lord's heart in a unique way, feeling indescribable solidarity with God (just as he often experienced extreme isolation from humanity), being identified with Him in totality. This is reflected in the not infrequent cases in the book in which oracles in the first person seem to alternate between God and Jeremiah, sometimes indistinguishably, to the point that it is

> sometimes impossible to delineate where God ends, so to say, and the prophet begins (and vice versa).[16]

The Lord so filled Jeremiah's heart that God's tears flowed out of him. Remember in Jesus' day, some of the people thought Jesus was Jeremiah come back from the grave. When Jesus asked His disciples who the people thought He was, one reply was, *"Some say you are Jeremiah."* (Matthew 16:14) Quite a commentary on Jeremiah's godliness! Listen to the pain of God portrayed in this book:

> *Why have they provoked Me to anger with their carved images—with foreign idols? Oh, that my head were waters, and my eyes a fountain of tears,* ***that I might weep day and night for the slain of the daughter of my people!*** *For they are all adulterers…they proceed from evil to evil, and they do not know Me, says the* LORD.
> (Jeremiah 8:19, 21; 9:1-3)

Behaving Like Donkeys in Heat

Our harlotry can remain unnoticeable for a long time because in many of us it only raises its ugly head when something comes along that we *really* want. I've seen some of the most seemingly spiritual believers throw their sanctification out the window when their secret idol suddenly crosses their path. I can see it in others because I've first seen it in myself. How can I describe it? The Lord likens it to a wild donkey in heat. How disgusting, but, according to Scripture, how fitting. God said through Jeremiah,

> *How can you say, "I am not polluted. I have not gone after the Baals"? See your way in the valley; know what you have done: You are a swift dromedary breaking loose in*

> *her ways,* ***a wild donkey used to the wilderness,*** *that sniffs at the wind in her desire; in her time of mating, who can turn her away?* ***For according to the number of your cities are your gods, O Judah...*** *You have forgotten Me and trusted in falsehood. Therefore I will uncover your skirts over your face, that your shame may appear. I have seen your adulteries and your lustful neighings, the lewdness of your harlotry, your abominations on the hills.*
> (2:23-24, 28, 13:25-27)

God was clearly frustrated with and very jealous over His people, as Michael Brown points out:

> Perhaps nowhere in Jeremiah—or perhaps the entire Bible—is the Lord's jealous indignation spelled out more clearly. God Himself is the One who has pulled Zion's skirts over her face, uncovering her before the world, shaming her in the most degrading way in the sight of her enemies, and thereby showing her off as an utter whore.[17]

Facing Our Idolatry

We can so easily and incorrectly echo Israel by saying, "*I am not polluted. I have not gone after the Baals.*" I was on staff at Times Square Church when David Wilkerson first preached about these wild donkeys in the book of Jeremiah. Jeremiah and David Wilkerson (and Michael Brown) are the only ones I've ever heard proclaiming the Lord's disgust over our idolatrous ways in such terms. Many of us have forgotten how to blush! (See Jeremiah 6:15, 8:12) We are also polluted, and we have gone after so many idols. I weep over my sins and the sins of the church, and I finally feel a release from the Lord to write about these truths that I have learned, digested, and made a part of my walk with Christ. Yes, if we commit idolatry while in covenant with God, the offence is adultery, spiritual adultery, spiritual whoredom which provokes the jealousy of a holy God.

We see through the words and lives of these five Old Testament prophets that Israel continually provoked her God to jealousy. Their spiritual adultery against God is one of the Bible's major themes, being the focus of most of the Old Testament prophetic messages. To use an analogy from art, the prophets painted their portraits of God's brokenhearted countenance on the canvas of the history of the nation of Israel, a history that has been written down for you and me to learn from today. So let's take a quick look through the historical books of the Bible.

PART TWO

HE'S JEALOUS OVER OUR IDOLATRY

CHAPTER 6

Vital Lessons From Israel's History

"These things happened to them as examples... written for our admonition."
—1 Corinthians 10:11

I've had the privilege of teaching Old Testament Survey classes in two Bible Schools: FIRE School of Ministry and Brooklyn Teen Challenge School of Ministry. In both classes I began with Paul's statements about Israel's failures in the wilderness, written to the believers in Corinth:

> *With most of them God was not well pleased, for their bodies were scattered in the wilderness. Now these things became our examples, to the intent that we should not lust after evil things as they also lusted.* ***And do not become***

> ***idolaters as were some of them....*** *Now all these things happened to them as examples, and they were written for our admonition.* (1 Corinthians 10:5-7, 11)

The generation that worshipped the golden calf at the base of Mt. Sinai ended up dying in the wilderness instead of inheriting their Promise Land. Paul's concluding statement was, *"Therefore, my beloved, flee from idolatry."* (v. 14) The emphasis here is on making sure we *"do not become idolaters,"* that we do not follow their example of worshipping idols.

If we are proud of the fact that we live in a nation that does not embrace idol worship, we should think again. As we look to the New Testament to define idolatry today, we can read its extremely expanded definition in two passages:

> *Put to death your members which are on the earth: fornication, uncleanness, passion, evil desire, and* ***covetousness, which is idolatry.*** (Colossians 3:5-6)

> *This you know that no fornicator, unclean person, nor* ***covetous man, who is an idolater,*** *has any inheritance in the kingdom of Christ and God.* (Ephesians 5:5)

Covetousness is idolatry and a covetous man is an idolater. Baker's Encyclopedia of the Bible says,

> To covet is to desire inordinately, to place the object of desire before love and devotion to God.[18]

The list of things we place before devotion to God is endless, so the list of possible idols is also endless! Here are some quotes from church leaders that echo this truth:

> As long as you want anything very much, especially more than you want God, it is an idol.[19] —A.B. Simpson

> What is an idol? It is anything more important to you than God, anything that absorbs your heart and imagination more than God, anything you seek to give you what only God can give.[20] —Tim Keller

> Idolatry is huge in the Bible, dominant in our personal lives, and irrelevant in our mistaken estimations.[21] —Os Guinness

We've taken a glimpse at the Old Testament prophetic books through the lives of Ezekiel, Isaiah, Hosea, Moses, and Jeramiah, seeing how prevalent idolatry was. As we take a quick look at the historical books in the Bible, what will come into focus is how huge and dominant idolatry always was (and still is). It wasn't just the wilderness generation that broke their covenant with God by falling into idolatry. It's every single generation.

Deuteronomy is most often remembered by the list of blessings God promised through Moses to the obedient and curses to the disobedient. The verse placed between the blessings and curses shows how they would basically either obey or disobey God. It says,

> *You shall not turn aside from any of the words which I command you this day, to the right or the left,* ***to go after other gods*** *to serve them.* (Deuteronomy 28:14)

Moses gives them stern warnings not to fall into idolatry lest the anger of the Lord come upon them and they be rooted out of the Promised Land. He forewarned them that their unfaithfulness would result in tragic consequences. (See Deuteronomy 29:24-28)

God mercifully gave them a new start in the land of Canaan. Not only did Joshua follow in the faithful footsteps of Moses, but also his warnings sound similar. He reminded them of God's faithfulness to all His promises, soberly adding that He would be just as faithful to punish them if they were to fall into idolatry (Joshua 24:20). Joshua didn't seem to have much confidence in the future faithfulness of God's people when he stated:

> *You cannot serve the LORD, for He is a holy God. He is a jealous God; He will not forgive your transgressions nor your sins. If you forsake the LORD and serve foreign gods, then He will turn and do you harm and consume you, after He has done you good.* (Joshua 24:19-20)

Because of the idolatry and gross immorality of the inhabitants of Canaan, the Lord instructed Israel to fully conquer and possess the land. But they didn't completely obey, and the nations around them became a snare to them. They soon intermarried with the Canaanites and learned their idolatrous ways. In the next historical book, Judges, we read,

> *They forsook the LORD God of their fathers, which brought them out of the land of Egypt,* ***and followed other gods,*** *of the gods of the people that were round about them, and bowed themselves unto them, and provoked the LORD to anger.* (2:12)

Just like God had warned, their sins brought chastisement in the form of oppression and slavery at the hands of nearby heathen nations. When their bondage became unbearable, the children of Israel would turn to the Lord and cry out to Him for mercy; only to turn away again after He delivered them:

> *The* L*ORD raised up judges who delivered them out of the hand of those who plundered them. Yet they would not listen to their judges,* ***but they played the harlot with other gods,*** *and bowed down to them.* (Judges 2:16-17)

The entire book of Judges can be summarized in these two verses:

> *It came to pass, when the judge was dead, that they reverted and behaved more corruptly than their fathers,* ***by following other gods,*** *to serve them and bow down to them... In those days there was no king in Israel; everyone did what was right in his own eyes.* (2:19; 21:25)

After the book of Judges, Israel stubbornly demanded that God allow them to be like the ungodly nations around them. They wanted a king, and they wanted one now! God reluctantly gave Israel their request, giving them a shepherd after their own heart. Israel's first monarch, King Saul, was just as stubborn and unfaithful to God as the people were. His sinful stubbornness caused Samuel to say to him:

> *Behold, to obey is better than sacrifice, and to hearken than the fat of rams. For rebellion is as the sin of witchcraft, and* ***stubbornness is as iniquity and idolatry.***
> (1 Samuel 15:23)

I've heard dozens of sermons regarding the fact that rebellion is as witchcraft, but it's just as true that stubbornness is as idolatry.

The next king of Israel, a man after God's own heart, loved the Lord so much that he never forsook Him for other gods. Perfect? No. Not even close. An idolater? Never! David, the beloved Psalmist of Israel, had a heart after God which we will examine closely later. His son, Solomon, although endued with incredible wisdom from heaven and blessed with a godly heritage, did not cultivate the same heart after God his father had. The Lord warned him that he had better choose to follow in the steps of his dad, but he didn't take heed:

> *If you walk before Me as your father David walked, in integrity of heart and in uprightness, to do according to all that I have commanded you... then I will establish the throne of your kingdom over Israel forever. But if you or your sons at all turn from following Me...* ***and go and serve other gods and worship them,*** *then I will cut off Israel from the land which I have given them.* (1 Kings 9:1-9)

What happened to this man of great wisdom, actually the wisest man on earth at the time? Nehemiah summarized the tragedy of Solomon's sinful choices:

> *You shall not give your daughters as wives to their [pagan] sons, nor take their daughters for your sons for yourselves. Did not Solomon king of Israel sin by these things? Yet among many nations there was no king like him, who was beloved of his God; and God made him king over all Israel.* ***Nevertheless, pagan women caused even him to sin.***
> (Nehemiah 13:25-26)

Solomon's downfall is told in detail in 1 Kings Chapter 11, one of the saddest chapters in the Bible, describing how he married numerous heathen women and built idol shrines in Jerusalem for them. Idolatry then became a permanent stain in the fabric of the nation. Soon afterwards, Solomon's kingdom was torn in two as judgment on his blatant and widespread idolatry. Jeroboam, a mighty warrior and one of Solomon's own men, encountered a prophet who symbolically rent his coat into twelve pieces, declaring,

> *Take for yourself ten pieces, for thus says the* Lord, *the God of Israel: "Behold, I will tear the kingdom out of the hand of Solomon and will give ten tribes to you...* ***because they have forsaken Me, and worshiped Ashtoreth the goddess of the Sidonians, Chemosh the god of the Moabites, and Milcom the god of the people of Ammon."***
>
> (1 Kings 11:31-32)

After Solomon died, Jeroboam ruled the ten northern tribes of Israel while the tribes of Judah and Benjamin became a separate nation. Although he was clearly told that idolatry caused Solomon's downfall, Jeroboam still followed in his ungodly steps. Rehoboam, the son of Solomon, reigned in Judah, but he didn't do much better. Then throughout the books of Samuel, Kings, and Chronicles we have the stories of a few good and many bad kings. Their downfall is summarized in 2 Chronicles:

> *All the leaders of the priests and the people transgressed more and more,* ***according to all the abominations of the nations,*** *and defiled [with idols] the house of the* Lord *which He had consecrated in Jerusalem...Therefore He brought against them the king of the Chaldeans.*
>
> (36:14, 20)

We see that the history of the nation of Israel is one of chronic unfaithfulness to their God. The ten northern tribes of Israel went into Assyrian captivity. Judah (and Benjamin) went into Babylonian captivity for seventy long and painful years.

CHAPTER 7

The Many Idols Just Beneath the Surface

"I am your shield, your exceedingly great reward."
—Genesis 15:1

Thus far, we have only touched upon outward, surface idolatry, a mere fraction of all the idols there were and still are today. As we explore this topic a little further, going deeper into the Scriptures, we will find idols hidden just beneath the surface. In the last chapter, we summarized **WHAT** happened to the children of Israel—from Moses to the end of Second Chronicles. In this chapter, we will look at **WHY** things happened by looking at two of the most influential idolaters in Israel's history, Solomon and Jeroboam, comparing them to faithful Abraham.

Abraham, Solomon, and Jeroboam

First, this is what the Lord said about Abraham:

> *The father of Abraham and the father of Nahor dwelt on the other side of the River [Euphrates] in old times;* ***and they served other gods.*** *Then I took your father Abraham from the other side of the River, led him throughout all the land of Canaan, and multiplied his descendants and gave him Isaac.* (Joshua 24:2-3)

The Lord spoke to Abraham right after he obediently arrived—as an at-risk immigrant—in a foreign land filled with hostile people. God assured him,

> *Do not be afraid, Abram. I am your shield, your exceedingly great reward.* (Genesis 15:1)

As with David, the Lord was his rock, his shield, his fortress in whom he found protection (See Psalm 18:1). King Solomon, on the other hand, looked to the wisdom of the world for his protection:

> *Solomon made a treaty with Pharaoh king of Egypt, and married Pharaoh's daughter; then he brought her to the City of David.* (1 Kings 3:1)

> The Faithlife Study Bible's comments on this verse are: The practice of marrying the daughters of neighboring rulers served as a peace treaty. While Solomon's reign represented a period of peace, foreign marriage alliances eventually caused the kingdom to crumble from within.[22]

> 1 Kings 11:1-4 says, *"King Solomon loved many foreign women, as well as the daughter of Pharaoh: women of*

> *the Moabites, Ammonites, Edomites, Sidonians, and Hittites—from the nations of whom the* Lord *had said to the children of Israel, 'You shall not intermarry with them, nor they with you.* **Surely they will turn away your hearts after their gods.'** *Then Solomon built a high place for Chemosh the abomination of Moab on the hill that is east of Jerusalem, and for Molech the abomination of the people of Ammon. And he did likewise for all his foreign wives, who burned incense and sacrificed to their gods."*

Many, if not most, of the foreign women Solomon married were for political reasons, sealing peace agreements so that he could enjoy an unprecedented reign of peace. That, and not God, was his shield. His plans worked, but at a very high moral cost. Some people will go to great lengths and extreme moral compromise to obtain "peace" in their homes, their marriages, their jobs, and even their ministries.

> *He had peace on every side all around him. And Judah and Israel dwelt safely, each man under his vine and his fig tree, from Dan as far as Beersheba, all the days of Solomon.*
> (1 Kings 4:24-25)

Yes, Solomon secured the peace he so diligently sought. But in doing so, his foreign wives' idol temples desecrated Jerusalem and Judah. It wasn't their false gods that Solomon was worshipping, but the peace those marriage-alliances purchased. Jeroboam, who had a front row seat to view Solomon's errors, still followed right in his ungodly steps. Why was that so? Jeroboam's idol was his position as a ruler among God's people. He would do anything to hold on to his place of prominence and security.

> *Jeroboam said in his heart, "If this people go up to do sacrifice in the house of the* L*ORD* *at Jerusalem, then shall the heart of this people turn again unto their lord, even unto Rehoboam king of Judah, and they shall kill me." Whereupon the king took counsel,* ***and made two calves of gold,*** *and said unto them, "It is too much for you to go up to Jerusalem: Behold thy gods, O Israel, which brought thee up out of the land of Egypt."* (1 Kings 12:26-30)

Although Jeroboam knew it was God who gave him his position as king, he would not trust the Lord to keep him there. Or to be more precise, whether God wanted him to remain ruler or not didn't matter all that much to him. He was willing to do whatever was necessary to keep his lot in life; and in so doing, he caused the nation to fall deeper into idolatry and immorality. If the people went to Jerusalem to worship, that could jeopardize his kingdom and his life. How many people "bow down" their standards to frantically keep the blessings they've actually received from the hand of a generous God? There's no indication that Jeroboam worshipped those silly golden calves he set up. He was worshipping his blessings, his God-given blessings!

Solomon certainly had more wives than he would ever need, so why keep adding to his huge harem? Daughters of foreign leaders secured the nation from being attacked by them. Solomon and Jeroboam sought security at all costs, even to the point of horribly disobeying their God. They did not allow the Lord to be their shield and their protector as Abraham certainly did.

King Saul's stubbornness was just as deep as Jeroboam's. He wanted the favor of his people even if that meant disobeying the direct commands of God to secure it. When we stubbornly want our own way, our desires have become more important to us than God's standards, God's Word, and God's will; and thus, our will has become our god. That's why the prophet Samuel declared to stubborn King Saul that *"stubbornness is as idolatry."*

Our hearts lean toward idolatry, our world is filled with idols, and this brief overview of the Old Testament confirms that this has always been so. Even so, what David Clarkson wrote (in 1864) is so true, even today:

> Though few will own it, nothing is more common [than idolatry].[23]

If we were to ask Solomon if he actually worshipped Chemosh the abomination of Moab or Molech the abomination of the people of Ammon, he would have said, "No way!" And King Jeroboam knew better than to actually bow down to the two golden calves of Samaria. But still, their root problem, which was hidden just below the surface, was idolatry.

> Idolatry isn't an issue; it is the issue. Deal with life on the glossy outer layers, and you might never see it; scratch a little beneath the surface, and you begin to see that it's always there, under some other coat of paint. There are a hundred million different symptoms, but the issue is always idolatry.[24]
>
> —Kyle Idleman

Receiving this prophetic view of both Old Testament history and how it corresponds to my Christian walk today is developing in me something overwhelmingly positive, a desire to become, like David, a man after God's own heart —instead of the nonchalant covenant-breaker I once was. I also am now able to rightly discern specks of idolatry in others, and God-willing (and if you are willing), I can see clearly enough to remove them from your eyes, as Jesus promised in the Sermon on the Mount.

CHAPTER 8

Removing My Planks and Seeing Your Specks

"You will see clearly to remove the speck from your brother's eye."
—Matthew 7:4

Jesus said, "Why do you look at the speck in your brother's eye, but do not consider the plank in your own eye? Or how can you say to your brother, 'Let me remove the speck from your eye'; and look, a plank is in your own eye? Hypocrite! First remove the plank from your own eye, ***and then you will see clearly to remove the speck from your brother's eye."*** (Matthew 7:3-4)

If we allow the Lord to remove the planks from our eyes, we then are in position to clearly see and help remove the specks in our brothers' eyes. As I have removed plank after plank after plank, I have come to agree with John Calvin and Kyle Idleman:

> Every one of us is, even from his mother's womb, a master craftsman of idols… The human heart is a perpetual idol factory.[25]

> Idolatry is the most discussed problem in the Bible… Because idolatry is the central problem of faith, it must be the central concern of all lovers of God and disciples of Jesus.[26]

Beloved, I'm convinced that there is as much idolatry in the hearts of us Americans as there was in the heathen Canaanites, and just as much in the Body of Christ today as in the land of Israel in the Old Testament. Because I think it will be helpful, I'll share with you the three most powerful idols that once plagued my heart.

My Idolatrous, Artistic Talents

Before I was a Christian, my identity was defined by my artwork. I won many contests in elementary, middle, and high school with my acrylic, watercolor, pastel, and especially my oil paintings. During the summer between 8th and 9th grades, my older sister Joyce encouraged me to take professional art lessons. Dad was completely against that. He insisted I get a summer job and forget the crazy idea of becoming an artist as a career. I don't know how Joyce pulled it off, but I took art lessons that summer. Although Dad was still very much against it, he allowed Joyce to pay for those lessons from the money she made through extra babysitting jobs. At Waverly

High School in the 10th grade, I had an accomplished oil painter as my Art Teacher, dear Mrs. Turner. Her paintings were absolutely beautiful. She encouraged me continually, and I soon painted a large picture of the famous gristmill at Hurricane Mills, Tennessee (across the street from Loretta Lynn's estate.) I really outdid myself. Even as a sophomore, I won first place in the annual high school art contest, a $200 scholarship from a local sponsoring bank, and to top it off, I immediately sold it for a good amount of money.

Mom and Dad came to the school one evening with me to see the exhibit. Dad stood in front of my painting which had a blue ribbon and a "sold" sign on it. (Perhaps being in real estate, it was the "sold" sign that got to him!) I can still see him in my mind's eye. He stood there for what seemed like an eternity with a stream of tears flowing down his face. He finally took off his glasses, wiped his face, and turned and hugged me, saying, "I'm so sorry. I was wrong. Joyce and you were right. You're an artist. I can't believe it; one of my sons is a real artist!"

A few weeks later Dad had a debilitating stroke and hardly talked again in the final days of his life. The last thing I remember Dad saying to me was his blessing on my artistic talents, sealing in my heart my identity as a genuine artist. After getting saved about six months later at the age of seventeen, I became twice as good and very proud of MY artwork. I was really good, and I knew it. My heart's desire was to become a world-famous Christian artist who not only would paint beautiful Tennessee landscapes, but also invent a whole new style of painting, focusing on luminous lighting. My ambitions were high. (And this was way before I ever saw a Thomas Kincade painting.)

I usually would work on four or five paintings at a time, always being consumed with my precious artwork. The man who led me to the Lord could see something that I could not or would not see: how idolatrous it all was to me. He tried telling me, but it was like water off a duck's back.

"I'll be sure to do it all for God's glory," was my pat answer. "I'll even paint Scripture verses on some of them." Then one day he informed me that someone accidentally set fire to all my finished paintings that I was storing in his apartment kitchen closet. I was furious, and that was weird because I hardly ever got mad; much less, furious. I rushed to the closet, swung open the door and found everything intact, just as I had left it the week before. I turned my dagger-filled eyes to my friend and yelled, "WHY DID YOU LIE TO ME? WHAT KIND OF CRUEL JOKE IS THIS?"

He very humbly replied, "I felt this was the only way to show you how much this art has become an idol to you." I was smitten with the truth. I could not deny it. Well, I guess I could have ignored it if I chose to. Instead, I sincerely prayed about it, and I heard the Lord very gently whisper to my waiting heart, "If I were to ask you to surrender your artwork to Me, would you?"

"Yes, Lord," was my sincere and immediate reply.

"Okay. Do it. Lay it all down. Surrender your plans, your identity, your idols, your all to the One who laid it all down for you on the cross."

I immediately got rid of every canvas, every tube of paint, all my brushes, easels, frames, and every art tool I owned (and there were many!). There was no angel stopping me on the top of this Mt. Moriah, but I have no regrets. Soon I was powerfully baptized in the Holy Spirit and God gave me a new and burning desire to preach the gospel of Jesus Christ as a missionary in New York City, the greatest mission field the world has ever known. That was over forty years ago and I've spent most of my adult life in the Big Apple.

Over the years, I've enjoyed designing book covers, brochures, and various graphics; but I can live without it. It's not my life and not my identity. But I know firsthand how idolatrous our artistic, musical, and creative talents can become. It's hard for a rich man (rich in money *or* talents) to enter the kingdom of heaven. (Matthew 19:23) We can get so wrapped up in OUR GIFTS, can't we? And I also know that God's plans for my life have far surpassed my original, petty, self-centered dreams.

Coveting a Spouse

Another powerful idol in my life has been marriage. Joyce Meyer nailed it when she said, "All the single sisters in the church are sad, and the married ones are mad!" You will be sad if the main goal in your life is to find a mate and you're still single. And once you find one, you'll soon be mad at your spouse for not living up to the unrealistic expectations you'll probably place on them.

In the first church I planted and pastored, both myself and my worship leader, Samuel Henry, were young (in our twenties) and single. I was ok with that until a friend told me of a conversation he had with my overseer, David Wilkerson.

"Pastor Dave told me that you will not be a successful pastor until you get married."

Well, that pierced my sensitive heart and set me on a collision course with disaster. A saintly old lady had told me months before, "God put Adam to sleep and when he woke up, presto, there was his wife. As far as a mate for you goes, keep sleeping and let God bring you the Eve He has for you in His perfect timing." Great advice. I took it to heart—until I heard Pastor Dave's comments. (Looking back, I can see that I began coveting a spouse because I was coveting ministerial success!)

The very next day, the most sold-out believer in my church told me she was going to invite a friend to next Sunday's service whom she KNEW was gonna be my wife! Soon Maria and I were friends. (I've changed her name since I will share some negative things about her.) There were numerous red flags about her which I either couldn't see or didn't want to.

One evening, an elderly sister from a nearby Spanish Pentecostal church attended our service and then lingered around afterwards. When only a handful remained in the sanctuary, she walked up to me and said, "The Lord sees your heart and your desire to follow Him completely, so He sent me here tonight to warn you of the wolf who is about to destroy your ministry." She glanced over at Maria who was impatiently waiting for me at the back door and said, "Don't you dare marry her or she will destroy your ministry." Oh my! Two very different opinions from two different believers. One thing for sure, I'd better pump the brakes!

I did put the brakes on my relationship with Maria. A few weeks later an associate pastor from Brooklyn Tabernacle called me. "Pastor Charles, I saw you and Maria at an evening service here last week."

"Yes, Pastor." I nervously replied. "And...?"

"Well, has Maria told you that she spent time in a mental hospital recently?"

"No."

"So, I'm sure she hasn't told you that when she was discharged, she moved in with one of the male doctors she met while she was there."

"No, Pastor. This is all new to me."

"She will destroy your ministry if you marry her," he bluntly concluded.

"Thank you for your advice. I appreciate it," and I hung up, realizing the same phrase was used twice. "...destroy your ministry." As gently as I could, I backed away from her.

I've seen too many believers marry too quickly, marry an unbeliever, or marry someone with a questionable character (including almost me). In all these situations, marriage had first become an idol. Time and time again, I've seen some of the most sanctified believers wildly chase after the idol of having a mate. If your sinfulness led you into a disastrous marriage, don't sinfully run away now. God is in the business of redeeming all our messes if we let Him. Tim Keller observed,

> If you marry someone expecting them to be like a god, it is only inevitable that they will disappoint you. It's not that you should try to love your spouse less, but rather that you should know and love God more.[27]

After pastoring for decades, I have found myself lamenting, "Why are so many believers deceived into marrying unsaved people when the Scriptures clearly forbid it?"

> *A wife is bound by law as long as her husband lives; but if her husband dies, she is at liberty to be married to whom she wishes,* ***only in the Lord.*** (1 Corinthians 7:39)

Can it be any clearer? Free to marry anyone… anyone in the Lord, that is, a believer. When marriage becomes an idol, moral standards are compromised to obtain it and discernment is forfeited in the process. Spiritual blindness is the result of idolatry. No wonder God is so against it. As I examined the near-disaster I almost made by marrying a dear sister who was clearly very mentally challenged, I realized the root cause of such deception was the idol of ministry success.

The Various Idols of Ministry

I've heard so many speak about their ministry as though it was the most important thing on the planet. Some TV evangelists desperately beg for money in hopes that the tragedy of the century would be averted—the collapse of their ministry. God would rather their ministry fold than for His Name to be dishonored by idolatrous men who will do almost anything to protect it from extinction. Some ministers have built empires around themselves. So often, their church becomes more important than the individual members who make up their congregation. Blaise Pascal observed that,

> People imagine they are pursuing the glory of God when actually they are only pursuing their own.[28]

Of the many ministers I've known in the last forty years, relatively few have exhibited freedom from ministerial idolatry. How can I make such a bold statement? I've allowed the Lord to severely judge me regarding idolatry, and now, just as He promised in Matthew 7:3, I can clearly see the specks in others.

A pastor who worships idols will have idol-worshippers in his congregation. We, like trees, bear fruit after our own kind whose seed is in itself. Just as it was in the days of Kings and Chronicles, whenever idol shepherds ruled, idolatry became rampant. Some of our dear leaders in the body of Christ are worshipping both God and Baal, God and their ministry, and this has not produced good fruit. "Ministry" too often is raised to the level of deity. Ministry and God are not the same things. John White compares David sinfully counting Israel with ministers today who allow their ministries to become the main focus of their lives:

> David paid a terrible price for his egocentric headcount of Israel. And somewhere along the lines many Christian evangelists and churches have done the same. Nobody could tell you when or how it happened, but little by little the church becomes important in and of itself.[29]

Our ministries are to be an overflow of our relationship with Christ. If it ever becomes more important to us than spending time with Jesus, it has become an idol. My wife shared with me that in the early years of her walk with God, she was begging Him to call her into "the ministry." He then asked her the piercing question, "Is it ministry, or is it Me that you want?" Some Christians focus so much on their ministry that they don't have time to pray so that God can birth a deep compassion for people in their hearts. God gives the desire, not necessarily to have a ministry, but to be a minister in the truest sense of the word—which is to be a servant: a servant to Christ, to fellow believers, and to the lost.

A successful ministry can become more important than being godly and walking in integrity. Making church growth, the development of an awesome social media platform, or relevance to our culture our main goals can easily cause us to compromise integrity. There's a place to be relevant, especially when it's birthed out of compassion for the lost. But honestly, too many of us have sacrificed the holiness of God on the altar of being relevant to our corrupt and idolatrous society. Raymond Ortlund comments:

> More than our showing the world how 'relevant' the church can be, God wants us to show Him how much we treasure Him above all else.[30]

Simon of Samaria so desperately wanted to be in the ministry of getting people filled with the Holy Spirit that he was willing to pay whatever amount of money he needed to do so![31] Some of us seek the anointing of the Holy Spirit for the wrong reasons. Our hearts are not right if we want to be acknowledged, like Simon, as the Great One. Michael Brown speaks of being caught up with the "peripherals" that surround working for the Lord:

> You may enjoy the forms of worship—good music, singing, maybe dancing, being part of an exciting corporate experience—but what about the object of worship? What about the Lord? You may have a vision. You may be caught up in a movement. You may have a message or a burden. Theology may intrigue you. Spiritual issues may interest you. The ministry may consume you. But all these things are mere idols and distractions in comparison with coming into the light of God's presence and fellowshipping with Him.[32]

What Is Your Pet Idol?

Is it your position? Your family? Your blessings? Your drug of choice? What's in your heart that competes for the adoration, attention, and affection that belongs exclusively to Christ? What are your golden calves? By asking the right questions regarding Solomon and Jeroboam we were able to uncover idolatry lurking just below the surface. Kyle Idleman in *Gods at War, Defeating the Idols that Battle for Your Heart*, lists pertinent questions to ask ourselves, designed to help diagnose where our heart is and what false gods (idols) might be receiving our undo worship:

1. What disappoints you?
2. What do you complain about?
3. Where do you make financial sacrifices?
4. What worries you?
5. Where is your sanctuary? (Where you go when you're hurting?)
6. What infuriates you?
7. What are your dreams?[33]

Since idolatry is a matter of the heart, what is an idol to one can mean nothing to another. We can and do make an idol out of just about anything and everything.

CHAPTER 9

American Idols

"According to the number of your cities are your gods."
—Jeremiah 2:28

Besides the three idols that I mentioned that once plagued me (my talents, marriage, and ministry) I am going to mention a few other common idols. For those of you still trying to pinpoint (or avoid) your specific idols, perhaps this list will be helpful (in alphabetical order): Businesses and Careers, Family, God-Given Dreams and Visions, Money, Our Blessings, People, Pleasure, Politicians, Religious Traditions, Sports, and The American Dream.

BUSINESSES AND CAREERS: David Clarkson wrote:

> Let your hearts be especially jealous of lawful comforts; these are the most dangerous snares. Because we may

> lawfully follow our callings and business, therefore men take liberty to follow them too eagerly, engage their minds and hearts too far upon them.[34]

Some have made their careers into idols to the point of sacrificing the welfare of their children (and sometimes even their unborn children) for the sake of their cherished professions. It mirrors the Canaanite practice of casting their children into the fire as they worshipped Molech.

FAMILY: There are people who worship their family members with the type of adoration that's appropriate only for our Creator. I'm aware of the fact that some of us need to care more, instead of less, about our loved ones. The sad truth is, however, that people can love father, mother, son, or daughter more than they love the Lord. (See Matthew 10:37)

God blessed Eli, the High Priest in First Samuel with two sons, and yet Eli placed his sons above the Lord when he would not sufficiently restrain their sinfulness. (They habitually fornicated with the women who came to the tabernacle!) The Lord asked Eli in 1 Samuel 2:29, "*Why do you… honor your sons more than Me?*" Why? Because his god was his children, the sons that God had given him! The gifts God gave to Eli became idols in his heart. Not only good things, but even God-given gifts can become idols we inwardly worship. Even something as precious as our families can become more important to us than the One who gave them to us. Francis Frangipane's comments are relevant:

> I must not let any relationship challenge His love and call upon my life. And, if there is a decision to be made about doing His will, I must always choose Him above

> everyone else's interests, even my own. By comparison, every other relationship I have could appear like hate when measured by my love and obedience to Jesus. Of course, loving Jesus brings the very best of heaven into all my other relationships; I possess something of Christ's life that brings greater love back to my family and friends, and even my own soul.[35]

GOD-GIVEN DREAMS AND VISIONS: Good things, even God-given things like the dreams He places inside us, can take such prominence in our lives that they take the place reserved for our God alone. Yes, even our life's vision given to us by God can become our idol. Paul Johansson wrote,

> We must be aware that sometimes our dreams and visions—even God-given ones—can become idols. Simply put, an idol is anything that takes preeminence above my relationship with God.[36]

I have been guilty of placing my calling of pastoring and church planting before my relationship with the One who called me to these things! Pastor Johansson shows how we can determine if our vision has become an idol:

- When my primary focus in life is my vision, rather than my relationship with God—it is an idol.
- When I can't die to my vision—it is an idol.
- When my present happiness and fulfillment are postponed until my vision is realized—it is an idol.

MONEY: Jesus said that we cannot serve two masters at the same time. We can't serve both God and money. How many people have bowed down their moral standards to obtain financial success? Like the rich young ruler, there are people who have idolized money and the things that money can buy to the point of walking away from the Lord; just like he did. The love of money truly is, *"a root of all kinds of evil."* (1 Timothy 6:10)

OUR BLESSINGS: Abraham wouldn't allow anything or anyone to become more important to him than his beloved Lord. He was even willing to offer up his son Isaac in obedience to God. This was an act of worship from a man who refused to idolize even the blessings given to him from heaven.

> *Abraham stretched out his hand and took the knife to slay his son. But the Angel of the Lord called to him from heaven and said, "Abraham, Abraham!" So he said, "Here I am." And he said, "Do not lay your hand on the lad, or do anything to him; for now I know that you fear God, since you have not withheld your son, your only son, from Me."*
>
> (Genesis 22:10-12)

We should also be willing to (figuratively) "put the knife to" anything God tells us to. Also, we need to be sure to hear the Lord tell us, *"Do not lay your hand on the lad!"* In other words, once God has given back those things we have been willing to sacrifice to Him, we then need to take care of them. (If He gives them back; if not, He has even better things for us. I know this firsthand.) Abraham's way of pleasing God, now that Isaac was returned, would be to raise his son in the nurture and admonition of the Lord. If he would have taken his son back to Mount Moriah every few months, (to prove that he still was sold out) Isaac would have grown up with an unnecessary, inferiority complex. Once our blessings have been laid on the altar and God gives them back to us, we can enjoy them and care for them in even greater depths than before. As long as God is first, we can fulfill our callings and ministries, loving and caring for our families and enjoying the blessings He bestows, doing it all unto the Lord.

PEOPLE: People are constantly made into idols on every level of society. There are some who ignore the call of God on their lives because they have chosen to listen to a loved one who disagreed with that calling. There are people who live their entire lives with the sole purpose of trying to win acceptance from their parents, sometimes even their deceased parents! This nation is filled with celebrities (stars from television, the music industry, sports, and even celebrity pastors) who are venerated as if they were superhuman gods. Many of them love to be worshipped and the unsaved undoubtedly love to adore them. Judson Cornwall said,

> We love our heroes, even our religious heroes, and we find it difficult to deny our heroes the status of divinity.[37]

Another aspect of idolizing people is called relational idolatry. Some people focus their whole life on finding that one person who will, so they think, complete them. When we fill our need for love primarily with someone God has made instead of God Himself, we're in danger of following those who "*...worshiped and served created things rather than the Creator.*" (Romans 1:25) Relational idolaters view another person as the source of their identity, security, and/or well-being. Andy Comiskey points out the root problem in this type of idolatry:

> In Romans 1:16-32 the Apostle Paul describes the human tendency to suppress the truth of God and to unite with illusions. Humanity tends to create its own gods and

> goddesses. One furtively seeks security in another… our wounds and deprivations are often at the core of our idolatrous yearnings and actions… Many bypass the Creator and their own true selves by seeking completion in another.[38]

This is often the root cause of sexual relationships that are contrary to Biblical values, such as lesbianism, homosexuality, and fornication (sex outside of marriage).

PLEASURE: King Herod chose to enjoy the pleasures of sin rather than repent when John the Baptist rebuked him for his adulterous relationship:

> *Herod had laid hold of John and bound him, and put him in prison for the sake of Herodias, his brother Philip's wife, because John had said to him, "It is not lawful for you to have her."* (Matthew 14:4)

Pleasure, especially sexual pleasure outside the Biblical parameters of marriage (which God has set for our good), is a damnable idol to many. Their philosophy is expressed in an old pop song that says, *"If loving you is wrong, I don't wanna be right."* Baltasar Gracian y Morales, the sixteenth century philosopher said, *"All men are idolaters, some of fame, others of self-interest, most of pleasure."*[39]

POLITICIANS: Why is our nation so viciously divided politically nowadays? I think the book of Acts holds the answer. When Paul's message threatened the lucrative idol industry of the Ephesians, the people came into the theater and screamed for two hours. They were that angry. When we idolize our politicians, political parties, or political agendas, then anything or anyone opposing them are therefore seen as our evil enemies who might threaten our livelihood; thus worthy of our wrath. Dr. Carl Ellis, Jr. in the article, *What Happens When Politics Drive Our Faith?* explains what happens when the church submits to politics more than to God's Word:

> Anyone who allows their politics to drive their faith is an idol worshiper. I will put it straight like that. The Kingdom of God is not determined by politics… God is above all of that. He calls us as Christians to have a voice not determined by conservatism, liberalism, Democrats, or Republicans. We should speak the truth of God's word to both sides.[40]

RELIGIOUS TRADITIONS: Many people worship their religious traditions. Certainly, there's a place for loyalty, but often we so venerate our traditions, that in doing so we *"make the Word of God of no effect by our traditions."* (Matthew 15:6) To some Christians (and this amazes me) it makes no difference if things are in God's Word or not. If it's not part of their tradition or denomination, they don't want anything to do with it. God doesn't want us to worship our past no matter how glorious it was.

We so easily become like the children of Israel who worshipped the instruments God used to bless them. In the book of 2 Kings, we see them idolizing the very thing that Moses had once used to bring God's healing to them, namely the bronze serpent. (See 2 Kings 18:4) Our idolatrous religious traditions can also include our cherished beliefs and even our own morality, as Tim Keller noted:

> Idolatry functions widely inside religious communities when doctrinal truth is elevated to the position of a false

> god. This occurs when people rely on the rightness of their doctrine for their standing with God rather than on God himself and His grace. It is a subtle but deadly mistake… Another kind of religious idolatry has to do with moral living itself… Though we may give lip service to Jesus as our example and inspiration, we are still looking to ourselves and our own moral striving for salvation… Making an idol out of doctrinal accuracy, ministry success, or moral rectitude leads to constant internal conflict, arrogance, and self-righteousness and oppression of those whose views differ.[41]

Some people who are obstinate and unyielding are that way because they think they are called to be in control of God's people and God's church. They are sadly mistaken. Spiritual leaders are to give oversight, but we are not to be in control, controlling people and meetings and situations according to our will. Rick Joyner, founder of Morningstar Ministries, wrote,

> After more than fifty years of full-time ministry around the world, I would say 90 percent of the Church in America is controlled by the religious spirit and not the Holy Spirit.[42]

SPORTS: Following our favorite sports team or sports celebrities can easily consume the attention of our hearts and grow into a full-fledged idol. Some believers know more details about their sports team than they know about their Bibles. Once, when the New York Yankees were in the playoffs, I cut a church service I was leading short so I could get home in time to watch it (and I have a DVR!). If you fall into a deep depression when your team is knocked out of the playoffs, that could be an indication that it means too much to you. Some men worship their sports teams because they're looking to that as their main source of excitement and pleasure in life, instead of finding it in God, the most exciting Person there is. The Lord calls us to live on a higher level than to look primarily to the entertainments of this world for our pleasure.

> Leonard Ravenhill wrote, "Entertainment is the devil's substitute for joy. The more joy you have in the Lord, the less entertainment you need."

> The Psalmist David said, *In Your presence is fullness of joy; at Your right hand are pleasures forevermore.*
>
> (Psalm 16:11)

We so easily can worship at the altars of sports, music, art, education, and a hundred other seemingly "innocent" things.

THE AMERICAN DREAM: Many of us are guilty of worshipping "The American Dream." This is when the goal in life is to own a home in suburbia or wherever we think we will be "happy." Certainly, there is nothing wrong with personal happiness and prosperity, but if that is our main goal in life, then it has become our god. I have seen believers who literally cherish their material blessings, mistakenly assuming "things" will fulfill them. But only God can fulfill us. Thus, He is jealous for us.

We can so easily and incorrectly proclaim like the people in Jeremiah's day, *"I am not polluted. I have not gone after the Baals."* But we are also polluted, and we have gone after so many idols. In conclusion, I see three definite, scriptural ways to identify when our hearts are going after idols (the ones listed above and others):

1. When we fall into covetousness (over anyone or anything), the Scriptures say that we are guilty of idolatry.

2. When we're willing to lower our standards to get or keep something, spiritually we are bowing down to an idol.

3. When we become sinfully stubborn, we have caused self-will to become our idol because stubbornness is as iniquity and idolatry. (1 Samuel 15:23)

When God puts His convicting finger on our idols, if we're not ready and willing to let go, anger will sometimes be the reaction, as in Ephesus (See Acts 19:28). When Paul came against their idolatry, the citizens were filled with wrath. It was the obstinate people of God who stoned the prophets who were sent to turn them away from their destructive idolatry. Whether the people will hear or not, God in His compassion persistently raises up prophetic voices, calling us from our broken cisterns that can hold no water, back to the eternal Fountain of Living Water. (Jeremiah 2:13)

The Lord's desire and design in sending His prophets filled with His heart and His Word is to bring forth the response of total, heart-felt repentance. Sometimes His people listen and repent; other times we don't listen at all. But often we do the very worst thing possible: repent with part, but not with all of our hearts, as in the days of Ezra.

CHAPTER 10

Ezra: From Bitter Captivity to Right Back into Bondage?

"Should we again break Your commandments?"
Ezra 9:14

Although Babylonian captivity did forever purge the Jewish people from outward idol worship, still the inward inclination was ever present. The people who returned from Babylon in the third century before Christ quickly set themselves up to fall into the same sins that brought on their captivity in the first place by marrying the idolatrous heathen around them. We see this in the book of Ezra. As soon as he reached Jerusalem from Babylon, we read:

> *The leaders came to me, saying, "The people of Israel and the priests and the Levites have not separated themselves*

from the peoples of the lands…For they have taken some of their daughters as wives for themselves and their sons, so that the holy seed is mixed with the peoples of those lands. Indeed, the hand of the leaders and rulers has been foremost in this trespass." [Ezra then prayed,] "O my God, I am too ashamed and humiliated to lift up my face to You…. ***Should we again break Your commandments, and join in marriage with the people committing these abominations?"*** (Ezra 9:1, 2, 14)

Why was it so wrong for them to marry Canaanites? As Nehemiah dealt with this same problem, he tells why breaking this part of the Covenant was so dangerous:

In those days I also saw Jews who had married women of Ashdod, Ammon, and Moab. So I contended with them… saying, "You shall not give your daughters as wives to their sons, nor take their daughters for your sons or yourselves. ***Did not Solomon king of Israel sin by these things?*** *Yet among many nations there was no king like him, who was beloved of his God; and God made him king over all Israel. Nevertheless pagan women caused even him to sin."*

(Nehemiah 13:23-31)

God is certainly not against interracial marriage. But heathen wives caused Solomon to fall into idolatry even though he had been granted an enormous amount of wisdom. If these Israelites followed Solomon's disobedient steps, it would only be a matter of time before the whole nation would, once again, be wallowing in idolatry. But didn't they remember the consequences of their past idolatry? They had just returned from a painful seventy-year captivity in Babylon because of it!

Only a remnant returned to the Promised Land. Only a small part of the entire nation was willing to leave Babylon, which was filled with idolatry. This is a picture of someone only partially or temporarily delivered from the besetting sin of idolatry. Most of the regathered Jews quickly were heading right back to their forefather's sinful ways. Although the people seemed to follow Ezra's example of sincerely grieving over their sins, they didn't have the same heart for God that he did.

When the Lord began to show me all the idols in my heart, I responded to His Spirit and truly repented the best I knew how. I determined never again to go after other gods. However, to my amazement, within a few short weeks my weak heart wandered away once again. I was still going to church, praying (somewhat mechanically), reading my Bible, having "devotions," and doing all the right outward things. But inwardly? The thoughts and affections of my heart wandered away from *"sincere and pure devotion to Christ."* (2 Corinthians 1:3 NASB)

It was then I became aware that the reasons for some of my past years of captivity and cruel bondages (yes, as a believer!) were due to various degrees of idolatry. Even so, I would find myself following Israel's example of heading right back into idol-producing situations as seen in the book of Ezra. For instance, I found it very hard to not make the churches I've planted the main focus of my life. (I'm sure every church planter knows what I'm talking about and how easy it is to idolize our ministries!) Corrie Ten Boom once commented about holding everything loosely in her hands because she knew if she grasped things too tightly, the Lord might have to pry her fingers open. She said,

> Hold everything in your hands lightly, otherwise it hurts when God pries your fingers open.[43]

When we live with open hands, God doesn't have to pry open our fingers. If someone would have told me years ago that I was guilty of the sin of idolatry, I would have strongly protested. However, now that the Lord is removing the planks from my eyes, I must acknowledge how often I've sinned in this manner. I also can see specks of idolatry ensnaring many believers today. At the point of being in the place of Ezra's people (falling right back into past patterns as soon as I came out of my last season of captivity), I had a decision to make. I could go in one of four directions.

Four Possible Responses to My Exposed Idolatry

1. I could **PRETEND** I had the victory over the idolatry in my heart as they did in Jeremiah's day: *"I am not polluted; I have not gone after the Baals."* (Jeremiah 2:23)

2. I could decide to **WATER DOWN ITS SINFULNESS** and just live in endless cycles of reverting back to idolatry, coming under oppressive bondages, and crying out to the Lord for deliverance over and over again like in the book of Judges: *"The LORD raised up judges who delivered them out of the hand of those who plundered them. Yet they played the harlot with other gods."* (Judges 2:17)

3. I could **TRY IN MY OWN STRENGTH** to overcome idols and try to become holy by fencing myself in, barricading myself from everything outwardly unclean like the Pharisees did: *"Woe to you, scribes and Pharisees, hypocrites! For* ***you cleanse the outside of the cup and dish,*** *but inside they are full of extortion and self-indulgence."* (Matthew 23:25)

4. Or I could **CRY OUT TO GOD FOR THE GRACE NEEDED** to overcome the deep propensity that we all have towards idolatry so that I will no longer provoke Him to jealousy.

The problem with choosing numbers 1, 2, or 3 is the fact that God is a Persistent Lover and a Persistent Pursuer. As persistent as we pursue our idols, God is even more persistent to win our hearts for Him! When Israel rationalized the sinfulness of their idolatrous ways, or pretended they were being faithful to Him, or became steeped in suffocating self-righteous legalism, God would not let them wander off too far before responding. Sometimes the response of a prophetic word was sufficient. Sometimes a strong and shocking prophetic rebuke would be enough to cause them to turn back to Him. Sometimes a season of Babylonian-like captivity only produced shallow repentance. Sometimes God has to hedge us in with afflictions to get our attention and fully wake us up spiritually, as He did with Hosea's wandering wife:

> *Behold,* ***I will hedge up your way with thorns,*** *and wall her in, so that she cannot find her paths. She will chase her lovers, but not overtake them; Yes, she will seek them, but not find them. Then she will say, "I will go and return to my first husband, for then it was better for me than now."*
>
> (Hosea 2:6-8)

I know of some believers who speak of their current idols with a very flippant attitude. But I spent too much time sitting under one of the Jeremiah-type prophetic voices of our day (David Wilkerson) to be so nonchalant about spiritual mistresses. That would be like naming to your wife the girls on your job that you have flirted with (or worse) in the past week! God calls our covetousness idolatry, and our idolatry spiritual adultery—against Him!

It's one thing to repent of the latest idol we were recently caught bowing down to (or bowing down our standards to get or keep), and it's quite another thing to overcome an idolatrous heart. The regathered Israelites, although they forsook outward idols, still had a deep tendency toward idolatry in their hearts. They had left Babylon, but Babylonian ways had not left them. Though Ezra totally repented, the nation as a whole did not.

Then God's people went through 400 years of prophetic silence between Malachi and Matthew. When the curtain was raised on the stage of the New Testament world, it was a very different one than Ezra's, much like the United States has dramatically changed since our founding fathers lived here over 400 years ago. It's interesting to discover that the birthing of the Pharisee movement during the intertestamental period came from a group called the Hasidim, the purified ones, a group fiercely determined to preserve the purity of the Jewish people. When we try to stay pure from idolatry on our own strength, we either miserably fail, or we miserably succeed; succeeding to the point that we do become outwardly pure—and are very inwardly proud about how spiritual we are. Sadly, I too have been there and have done that.

By the time Jesus arrived on the scene, much of the nation of Israel did forsake every idol except one—the most powerful one, the one a prophet named John the Baptist thundered against: the idol of self.

CHAPTER 11

John the Baptist: The Idol of Self

"The axe is laid to the root of the trees."
—Matthew 3:10

Warren Wiersbe noted:

> The Jewish nation was persistently guilty of idolatry. God's judgments on the false gods of Egypt did not make a lasting impression on Israel. The repeated chastening, recorded in the book of Judges, apparently effected no lasting cure. First, God chastened them in their land, and then God took them captive out of their land. That finally cured them.[44]

The regathered Jews, while purged from outward idolatry, were still not cured inwardly. What a dangerous place to be! Jesus called it being empty, swept and garnished:

> *When an unclean spirit goes out of a man, he goes through dry places, seeking rest, and finds none. Then he says, "I will return to my house from which I came." And when he comes, he finds it* ***empty, swept, and put in order*** *(KJV, garnished). Then he goes and takes with him seven other spirits more wicked than himself, and they enter and dwell there; and the last state of that man is worse than the first.* ***So shall it also be with this wicked generation.***
>
> (Matthew 12:43-45)

That sinful generation was likened to a house that was swept clean, but very empty. They didn't raise up the old idols of the past, yet Jesus said they were an adulterous generation, referring to their spiritual condition before God.

> *He said to them, "An evil* ***and adulterous generation*** *seeks after a sign, and no sign will be given to it except the sign of the prophet Jonah."* (Matthew 12:39)

Yes, Babylonian captivity cured Israel of outward idolatry, but nature abhors a vacuum (I know from experience). Apparently, so did Theodore Parker who wrote, "*If a man worship not the true God, he will have his idols.*" If that void is not filled with true worship of God, the most dangerous and deadly idol of all will fill its place: the idol of self.

The Powerful Idol of Self

This is probably the most common idol of all, even among believers. Richard Cecil observed:

> The very heart and root of sin is an independent spirit. We erect the idol of self, and not only wish others to worship, but worship it ourselves.[45]

This was the idol of Adam and Eve. By deciding for themselves what was right and wrong, they essentially became their own gods, their own lords. Without a deep crucifixion to self, we can be freed from worshipping everything and everyone, and still not give our Lord wholehearted worship. Why? We're too busy admiring how well we're doing spiritually! Or we're too busy thinking about ourselves, negatively or positively, to focus much on God. A.W. Tozer wrote:

> Self is one of the toughest plants that grow in the garden of life. It is, in fact, indestructible by any human means. Just when we are sure it is dead, it turns up somewhere as robust as ever to trouble our peace and poison the fruit of our lives… The victorious Christian neither exalts nor downgrades himself. His interests have shifted from self to Christ. What he is or is not no longer concerns him. He believes that he has been crucified with Christ and he is not willing either to praise or depreciate such a man.[46]

Samuel Rutherford declared,

> What made Demas to go off the way of the Gospel, to embrace this present world? Even self-love and love of gain for himself. [2 Timothy 4:10] Every man blameth the devil for his sins; but the great devil, the house-devil of every man, the house-devil that eateth and lieth in every man's bosom, is that idol that killeth all: himself.[47]

I can testify firsthand to the power of this idol called self. When, in my walk with the Lord, I finally reached the place of being spiritually in the book of Ezra, I truly began mourning over my current idols and my deep tendency towards idolatry. When I determined never again to worship the ministry, or a man of God, or any other person or thing, the worship of self then began to flood my heart. Gone was the adoration of others, but in its place? Self-righteousness, self-pity, self-adoration, and other manifestations of self-worship.

God's people who do not fill their lives with worship will invariably become filled with self. Proverbs 14:14 says, "*The backslider in heart shall be filled with his own ways.*" The ax must be laid to the root in order to topple this powerful Dagon. (1 Samuel 5:13) The truth is, the regathered Jews were still idolaters in heart. Their inward self-righteousness, self-glorification, and self-confidence was so well hidden beneath the surface that it took the eyes of the prophet John the Baptist to see it. John didn't just come as a New Testament preacher, but also as a prophet, sent to prepare a people to receive the long-awaited Messiah. John the Baptist wore the same type of clothes that Elijah did, and had the same fervent heart for God, longing to see His people forsake their sins and turn wholeheartedly to Him. That's why John boldly exposed their hidden idols of self-worship. Notice what he said when the self-righteous Pharisees came to his baptism:

> *Brood of vipers! Who warned you to flee from the wrath to come? Therefore bear fruits worthy of repentance, and* **do not think to say to yourselves, "We have Abraham as our father."** *For I say to you that God is able to raise up children to Abraham from these stones. And even now* **the ax is laid to the root of the trees.** *Therefore every tree which does not bear good fruit is cut down and thrown into the fire.* (Matthew 3:7-10)

The ax being laid to the root refers to the fact that their root problem was their self-righteousness, self-centeredness, and self-adulation. They thought they needed no repentance simply because they were the children of Abraham. John the Baptist had to hit them hard because they were so deceived as to their true condition. Jesus later said to them,

> *Woe to you, scribes and Pharisees, hypocrites! For you cleanse the outside of the cup and dish, but inside* **they are full of extortion and self-indulgence...** *you are like whitewashed tombs which indeed appear beautiful outwardly, but inside are full of dead men's bones and all uncleanness. Even so you also outwardly appear righteous to men, but inside you are full of hypocrisy and lawlessness.* (Matthew 23:25-27)

Let me summarize and emphasize Jesus' description of them. They were *"full... of self."* This is seen in how they prayed:

> *The Pharisee stood and prayed thus with himself, "God, I thank You that I am not like other men—extortioners, unjust, adulterers, or even as this tax collector. I fast twice a week; I give tithes of all that I possess."* (Luke 18:11)

He mentioned "God" once, and "I" five times! Paul wrote with much anguish of heart about the sad tragedy that many of his beloved Jewish brethren had not submitted to the righteousness of God in Christ because they were, *"seeking to establish their own [self] righteousness."* (Romans 10:3) The reason why they were deceived as to their true condition is because they were not only empty and swept, but also garnished. To be garnished means to be decorated and adorned with only shallow, cosmetic changes. In other words, it means to improve the appearance without making any basic, structural changes. These people appeared to be worshippers of God, but they basically still were idolaters; now worshiping "self" instead of statues, and "I" instead of outward idols. They would never again raise up the idols of Canaan within their land, and they were extremely proud of this!

We too can pride ourselves in our lack of idolatry, and at the same time become avid worshippers of self. As we repent of our idols, let's be careful not to fall into this trap of becoming empty, swept, and garnished. Partial repentance will leave the deep-rooted idol of self still standing on the altar of our hearts. That was the spiritual condition of the nation of Israel, causing many of them to reject their Messiah when He walked into their world. Judson Cornwall wrote,

> Since the human heart is the same everywhere, it is likely that after we have done everything we can to destroy our idols and to return to pure worship of God, **we will eventually rebuild what we have destroyed unless there is a deep change in our hearts.** Some persons seem to spend their entire lives in a cycle of building idols, destroying idols, and rebuilding them again. The outer form changes, but the inner desire remains the same… few persons in our generation have developed the discipline to consistently refuse to return to their idols, no matter how meaningless they may have proved to be.[48]

The Expulsive Power of a New Affection

The gospel can bring deep change to our hearts, and the gospel is Jesus! He offers a deep and new affection! Thomas Chalmers in his famous sermon, "*The Expulsive Power of a New Affection*," taught from the parable of the treasure in the field that the treasure is worth joyfully selling all a man has to obtain it:

> *The kingdom of heaven is like treasure hidden in a field, which a man found and hid; and for joy over it he goes and sells all that he has and buys that field.* (Matthew 13:44)

Chalmers taught that for putting off the sin of idolatry to be effective, Christ must be perceived as the greatest treasure, the worthy object of our love:

> In a word, if the way to disengage the heart from the positive love of one great and ascendant object is to fasten it in positive love to another, then it is not by exposing the worthlessness of the former, but by addressing to the mental eye **the worth and excellence of the latter,** that all old things are to be done away, and all things are to become new.[49]

That requires a whole new reorientation of the heart upon a new love and a new passion, greater and deeper than our love for our former idols. While working in a drug rehab ministry for years now (Brooklyn Teen Challenge), I have seen these truths being walked out in the lives of former addicts who are now joyful new creations in Christ. Ed Welch correctly describes drug addiction as a worship disorder. He summarizes it this way:

> Life is about God. It is about worshipping Him, trusting Him, knowing Him, and loving Him. The deepest problem for addicts is that they are not worshipping, trusting, knowing, or loving the true God. Instead, they are running and hiding from God or rebelling against Him.[50]

David and Don Wilkerson, Co-Founders of Teen Challenge, may have been instrumental for the deliverance of more people from serious bondages than any other two people in the history of the church. Regarding this principle of "*The Expulsive Power of a New Affection*," Pastor Dave said:

> Certainly, we cannot claim a magical cure for addiction. The devil which hides in the needle, the pills, and the powder is so deadly strong that any such claim would be foolish. All we can say is that we have found a power that captures a person more strongly than narcotics; but He captures only to liberate.[51]

> Tim Keller noted: idols cannot simply be removed. They must be replaced… It is worship that is the final way to replace the idols of your heart—private prayer, corporate worship, and meditation.[52]

The power of God's love and His Holy Spirit are greater than the power of idolatry. For those who continued to listen to John the Baptist's preaching, they would be introduced to Jesus. "*Behold! The Lamb of God who takes away the sin of the world.*" (John 1:29) Let John's introduction of our Messiah sink in: "*The Lamb of God…*" the One who was wounded for our transgressions, bruised for our iniquities, and is still pierced by our unfaithfulness to Him.

PART THREE

THE TRANSFORMATION OF ISRAEL, AND US

CHAPTER 12

Zechariah: Beholding Israel's Pierced Messiah

"They will look on Me Whom they pierced."
—Zechariah 12:10

Zechariah is an Old Testament minor prophet whose prophecies stretch all the way to the very last days when we will see the full restoration of the nation of Israel. In Zechariah, Chapter 12 we read of a time when many nations will come against Israel with the intention of annihilating it. The nation as a whole will then turn to the Lord with all their hearts because of this real and imminent threat of extinction. As they cry out to Him, He will answer and intervene in fulfillment of Deuteronomy 4:30, 31:

> When you are in distress, **and all these things come upon you in the latter days,** when you turn to the Lord your God and obey His voice (for the Lord your God is a merciful God), He will not forsake you nor destroy you, nor forget the covenant of your fathers which He swore to them.

The Lord still has a covenant with the nation of Israel. They are still His chosen nation and *"the apple of God's eye."* (Zechariah 2:8) We've focused much on Israel's mistakes and failures because we are instructed by Paul to learn from them. There's a danger however, in seeing only the bad and thus giving a wrong impression. There's no place for even a trace of anti-Semitism in the hearts of those who follow Jesus Christ, the Jewish Messiah who has grafted us into the olive tree. So many of the spiritual blessings we have today, including the Word of God and our Saviour, we owe to the Jewish people. Jesus did say, *"Salvation comes through the Jews."* (John 4:22 NLT)

It's true that the nation collectively was cut off from God as stated in Romans 11. But what does that mean? Simply this: being a part of one nation (even being Abraham's descendants) will no longer assure you of God's blessing on your life. You now must, as an individual, accept God's Messiah. As far as salvation goes, all nations are now in the same condition—lost in sin and needing God's mercy. This has opened the door of opportunity for all the Gentiles to come to God along with the Jewish people. All must individually come to Christ in order to be saved. Regarding the Jews, Paul wrote, *"At the present time there is a remnant according to the election of grace."* (Romans 11:5) I take this to mean that God has graciously elected to save everyone (Jew and Gentile) who will call upon the Lord

Jesus. In Paul's day, many Jews (himself included) were saved by grace through faith in Christ. However, a time will come when the entire nation turns to the Lord:

> *And so all Israel will be saved, as it is written: "The Deliverer will come out of Zion, and He will turn away ungodliness from Jacob."* (Romans 11:26)

As many nations one day will try to destroy Israel, out of sheer desperation they will turn their hearts completely to the living God. I'm not an end time expert on how and when these events with Israel will play out. But even so, we can clearly see that the key to Israel's victory over idolatry is found in this passage. It's here we find Israel's deliverance from idolatry outlined:

> *In that day the Lord will defend the inhabitants of Jerusalem; the one who is feeble among them in that day shall be like David, and the house of David shall be like God, like the Angel of the* LORD *before them. It shall be in that day that I will seek to destroy all the nations that come against Jerusalem. And I will pour on the house of David and on the inhabitants of Jerusalem the Spirit of grace and supplication;* ***then they will look on Me whom they pierced. Yes, they will mourn for Him*** *as one mourns for his only son, and grieve for Him as one grieves for a firstborn. In that day there shall be a great mourning in Jerusalem.* (Zechariah 12:8-11)

Our Roadmap to Victory

In this prophetic passage, which is yet to be fulfilled, we have Israel's final deliverance from the besetting sin of idolatry. The nation will realize that the One they pierced and rejected,

Jesus of Nazareth, is their Messiah! Matthew Henry's comments on Zechariah 12 says,

> Those that truly repent of sin look upon Christ as One whom they have pierced, who was pierced for their sins and is pierced by them; and this engages them to look unto Him, as those that are deeply concerned for Him.

Yes, Jesus was pierced for our sins and by our sins. At the crucifixion, He took our punishment: **pierced for us**. When we sin, we are sinning against the Lord: **pierced by us.** The soldier at the cross pierced Jesus' side, in partial fulfillment of Zechariah's prophecy:

> *One of the soldiers pierced His side with a spear, and immediately blood and water came out.... these things were done that the Scripture should be fulfilled, "They shall look on Him whom they pierced."* (John 19:35, 37)

But this soldier did not repent. He was just making sure the next crucified man was truly dead. Look at what looking upon the Pierced One is able to produce:

> *They will look on Me whom they pierced. Yes, they will mourn for Him... In that day a fountain shall be opened for the house of David and for the inhabitants of Jerusalem, for sin and for uncleanness. It shall be in that day, says the* LORD *of hosts, that* ***I will cut off the names of the idols from the land,*** *and they shall no longer be remembered.*
>
> (Zechariah 12:8; 13:1, 2)

We look, we mourn, and we are cleansed! As we are delivered from sin and uncleanness, God will so enthrall us that we won't recall the things we once worshipped in His place.

But have we realized how much our sins have pierced the heart of Him who so dearly loves us? Have we looked upon Him Whom we have pierced? A parallel verse is Ezekiel 6:9:

> Then those of you who escape will remember Me among the nations where they are carried captive, **because I was crushed by their adulterous heart which has departed from Me,** and by their eyes which play the harlot after their idols; **they will loathe themselves for the evils which they committed** in all their abominations.

Here we see a people who:

1. see the pierced heart of God,
2. realize their sins against Him caused the piercing, and
3. deeply repent over what they have done to Him.

Charles Spurgeon wrote,

> We see the Lord pierced, and then the piercing of our own heart begins.[53]

What a day that will be when the nation of Israel beholds their Passover Lamb. What a revealing of the love of God and a revealing of their sins which pierced His loving heart. What an immediate softening and melting of hardened hearts! What an outpouring of grace, supplication, and cleansing that will take place then! A national outpouring of amazing grace…a whole nation resurrected to life from spiritual death!

> *For I speak to you Gentiles; inasmuch as I am an apostle to the Gentiles, I magnify my ministry, if by any means I may provoke to jealousy those who are my flesh and save some of them. For if their being cast away is the reconciling*

of the world, what will their acceptance be but life from the dead? (Romans 11:13-15)

This same type of revealing, repenting, and cleansing can be experienced by you and me today, as described in the New Testament Epistle of James (aka Jacob, Jesus' half-brother).

CHAPTER 13

James: Adulterers and Adulteresses!

"Adulterers and adulteresses! Do you not know that friendship with the world is enmity with God?"
—James 4:4a

The biblical truth that idolatry within God's people is spiritual adultery, while rooted in the Old Covenant, is also given to the church today. James makes this crystal clear. The Lord used him to shock the first century believers into the reality of how their unfaithfulness affected Him. In my opinion, James 4:4 is the strongest rebuke given to believers in the entire Bible.

> ***Adulterers and adulteresses!*** *Do you not know that friendship with the world is enmity with God? Whoever*

> *therefore wants to be a friend of the world makes himself an enemy of God.* (James 4:4)

James sounds like a condensed Jeremiah or Ezekiel or another Old Testament prophet.

> James's approach to ethical problems and his denunciations and warnings finds striking parallels in the Old Testament prophetical books. He appears as a kind of Christian prophet. (Guthrie)[54]

Commenting on James 4:4, Paul Copeland writes:

> When we choose this—worldly pursuits over our relationship with God, we engage in spiritual adultery which provokes God's righteous jealousy.[55]

The thing that is appalling here is not just our sinfulness, but rather the words that describe our wayward actions as "adulterous." Why does the Lord (through James) use the term adultery? Because when we gave our hearts to Christ, we came into a covenant relationship with Him, similar to a marriage vow (as Israel at Mount Sinai). We, as New Covenant believers, have come into union with Christ, a union even deeper than under the Old Covenant. As the heart of a bride belongs exclusively to her groom, so we belong to Jesus, our Bridegroom. Paul wrote,

> *You also have become dead to the law through the body of Christ, that you may be married to another—to Him who was raised from the dead.* (Romans 7:4)

Even just wanting to be a friend of this world makes us enemies of God! James throws no loose punches here. Raymond Ortlund writes,

> Each particular individual is bidden to search himself for the adultery of desiring the friendship of the world... And it is merely the desire for friendship with the world—not total immersion in it, or complete identification with it, but merely the wish to be on good terms—which draws a frown from God.[56]

Why is wanting the world's friendship so wrong? A great question which I'll let Paul Copeland answer:

> To be a "friend of the world" is to be on good terms with the persons and forces and things that are at least indifferent toward God, if not openly hostile to him. More fully... to savour the approval of those who disregard God and as a result grant favour according to godless criteria and for God-neglecting reasons—this, and much more, is friendship with the world.

Here in James' Epistle this message of spiritual adultery takes on a new aspect: the reality that, not just the nation of Israel as a whole and not just the entire church as a whole, but individual members individually commit spiritual adultery against our Lord when we are unfaithful to Him. My sins hurt Him. My idolatry provokes Him to jealousy. My adultery committed against Him crushes His heart! Paul echoed this individual relationship with our Groom when he encouraged the Corinthians to remain faithful to Christ. He had a godly jealousy over them, desiring to present them to the Lord as spiritually chaste virgins:

> *I betrothed you to one husband, that to Christ I might present you as a pure virgin. But I am afraid, lest as the serpent deceived Eve by his craftiness, your minds should*

> *be led astray from the simplicity and purity of devotion to Christ.* (2 Corinthians 11:2, 3, NASB)

This Scripture shows us that if we lose the purity of our devotion to Jesus, we are losing our spiritual virginity. This is how God sees it and the way He sees things is the way things truly are. (See Psalm 119:128) This means that covetous believers are more like harlots than pure brides awaiting their groom. Once these incredibly hard rebukes in James are received and we admit, "That's me, Lord. That's the condition of my heart," only then can we follow God's instructions given through James (which parallels Zechariah's), directing us to total deliverance from idolatry.

James' Parallel Roadmap to Victory

Where is the solution found? In the next verses:

> *Do you think the Scriptures have no meaning? They say that God is passionate that the spirit he has placed within us should be faithful to him.* ***And he gives grace generously.*** *As the Scriptures say, "God opposes the proud but gives grace to the humble." So humble yourselves before God. Resist the devil, and he will flee from you. Come close to God, and God will come close to you. Wash your hands, you sinners;* ***purify your hearts, for your loyalty is divided between God and the world.*** *Let there be tears for what you have done. Let there be sorrow and deep grief. Let there be sadness instead of laughter, and gloom instead of joy. Humble yourselves before the Lord, and he will lift you up in honor.* (5-10 NLT)

The Amplified Bible says in verse 8, *Recognize that you are sinners, get your soiled hands clean; realize that you have*

> *been disloyal wavering individuals with divided interests, and* ***purify your hearts of your spiritual adultery.***

God is promising in this passage to give us enough grace to overcome our tendencies towards idolatrous unfaithfulness. His grace is sufficient to enable us to overcome all things. Grace is more than divine unmerited favor. Grace includes God's "divine influence upon the heart and its reflection in the life."[57] His grace includes His enabling power. As Charles L. Allen said,

> In the Bible there are three distinctive meanings of grace; it means the mercy and active love of God; it means the winsome attractiveness of God; [and] it means the strength of God to overcome.[58]

More grace is what I need. And how is this obtained? *God gives grace to the humble.* (James 4:9) To humble ourselves the way James describes here begins with the word "submit:"

> *But He gives more grace. Therefore He says: "God resists the proud, but gives grace to the humble." Therefore submit to God.* (James 4:9, 10)

To submit to God is to submit to His Word. It is to take what James says about our sins as relevant and true. If God uses this message to show you something you've never known before—that your covetousness (aka idolatry) is spiritual adultery against God, and you humbly accept this truth, it will produce godly sorrow. This holy lamentation is given to us (like in the book of Zechariah) by the outpouring of God's grace and Spirit and His revelation to us of His Son… His pierced Son.

As we humble ourselves in the sight of the Lord, James wrote, *"He will lift us up,"* not necessarily up upon a platform where we're exalted in the eyes of men, but somewhere much more precious. He will lift us up into a place in Him where, by His grace we overcome idolatry and we become, in heart and soul, like David.

Yes, spiritual adultery takes place on the individual level. Not just Israel, and not just the church, but I have sinned against my God in this manner. But as I submitted to these truths, the other side of the coin began to dawn upon me: If my unfaithfulness breaks His heart, my faithfulness to Him must bless Him tremendously. Raymond Ortlund wrote:

> The marital nature of the covenant intimates [implies] **depths of communion with God** for which the human soul yearns amid the barrenness of the modern world.[59]

Since God wants me to be a faithful spouse to Him, then He also wants to relate to me in a deeper level of communion than I'd ever dreamed of; a communion that our souls long for, a communion that David, the sweet Psalmist of Israel, enjoyed and expressed through his psalms as he became a role model for us all.

PART FOUR

A GLORIOUS, VICTORIOUS CHURCH

CHAPTER 14

David: What is a Man After God's Own Heart?

"The one who is feeble among them in that day shall be like David."
—Zechariah 12:8

Zechariah's prophetic passage outlining total deliverance once and for all for the nation of Israel began with this promise:

> *In that day the* Lord *will defend the inhabitants of Jerusalem;* ***the one who is feeble among them in that day shall be like David.*** (12:8)

I believe this verse refers to the heart transformation that causes the spiritually feeble ones to become men and women who, like David, faithfully run after the heart of God. Will this Davidic company of last days believers (Jews and Gentiles) become the spotless and devoted bride our Jesus yearns for? David was, according to the Lord's description, a man after God's own heart.

> *Samuel said to Saul, "The* L*ORD has sought for Himself* ***a man after His own heart,*** *and the* L*ORD has commanded him to be commander over His people."*
>
> (1 Samuel 13:13-14)

But what exactly does that mean? I once overheard one man speaking about an acquaintance, "He likes pizza as much as I do. Yes, he's a man after my own heart!" This meant they were passionate about the same things. Although David did like the things God likes and hated the things that He hates, it goes deeper than personal likes and dislikes. David's heart went after, not only God's interests, but after the very heart of God Himself. David served the Living God Whom he knew has a heart that can be blessed or crushed by the actions of His people. When Israel was living in fine cedar houses, for instance, David began to be concerned about how God was doing and feeling:

> *It came to pass when the king was dwelling in his house, and the* L*ORD had given him rest from all his enemies all around, that the king said to Nathan the prophet, "See now, I dwell in a house of cedar, but the ark of God dwells inside tent curtains."* (2 Samuel 7:1-2)

No one in Scripture had ever spoken like that before, being so concerned about God as though He were a real Person (which He is). When David said in the Psalms, *"Bless the Lord, oh my soul, and all that is within me, bless His holy name!"* (Psalm 103:1) he knew his praises touched the Lord.

They actually put a smile on God's face and warmed His heart. They really did bless Him! David had his shortcomings, like all of us. But the one thing that made him stand out above the crowd was his total lack of ever indulging in any type of idol worship. He knew that if he indulged in idolatry he would be *"a-whoring from his God."* (Psalm 73:27 KJV) David refused to sin against his beloved Lord in that manner. He never had to turn from his wicked ways of idolatry because he never turned to them. (Yes, he sinned in other ways, but never with foreign gods.) David's heart was tried and found faithful and true to his Lord in this matter. He prayed,

> *You have tested my heart; You have visited me in the night; You have tried me and have found nothing.* (Psalm 17:3)

Even in the very hard seasons of his life, David could say,

> *All this has come upon us; but we have not forgotten You, nor have we dealt falsely with Your covenant. Our heart has not turned back, nor have our steps departed from Your way; but You have severely broken us in the place of jackals, and covered us with the shadow of death.* ***If we had forgotten the Name of our God, or stretched out our hands to a foreign god, would not God search this out?*** *For He knows the secrets of the heart.* (Psalm 44:17-21)

A man after God's own heart is also someone who wholeheartedly pursues the will of God for their lives. Peter said,

> *He raised up for them David as king, to whom also He gave testimony and said, "I have found David the son of Jesse,* ***a man after My own heart, who will do all My will."***
> (Acts 13:22)

David became the standard of a godly king for all who would follow after him. The kings of Israel and Judah are described as either walking in the idolatrous ways of Jeroboam or in the ways of David. Jeroboam idolized security, making golden calves in Bethel and Dan to insure he'd keep his job; attempting in his flesh to hold onto his God-given blessings. Many kings would follow his ungodly example in the years to come, while a few would follow David's example.

The Kings Who Followed David

JEHOSHAPHAT: "*...**walked in the former ways of his father David**; he did not seek the Baals but sought the God of his father... he removed the high places and wooden images from Judah.*" (2 Chronicles 17:3-5)

HEZEKIAH: "*...did what was right in the sight of the LORD, **according to all that his father David had done**. He removed the high places, broke the sacred pillars, and cut down the wooden images.*" (2 Kings 18:3, 6)

And then there was **KING JOSIAH:** "*...He did what was right in the sight of the LORD and **walked in the ways of his father David...** he began to purge Judah and Jerusalem of the high places, the wooden images, the carved images, and the molded images. They broke down the altars of the Baals... and made dust of them and scattered it on the graves of those who had sacrificed to them. He also burned the bones of the priests on their altars, and cleansed Judah and Jerusalem.*" (2 Chronicles 34:2-5)

We see from these examples that developing a heart after God and following David's ways means not only repenting and forsaking our idols, not just becoming a worshipper, but also a warrior! Those who followed David waged war against idolatry by (1) tearing down altars, (2) grinding them to powder, and (3) burning bones upon them. What do these three things signify to us today?

Tearing Down the Altars

It's our responsibility to tear down the idolatrous altars in our hearts once we become aware of them. It's our place to destroy them even if we have to rend our hearts to become free from their tenacious grips. (Joel 2:13 says, *"Rend your heart, and not your garments."*) Gideon was told that God would mightily use him, but the Spirit of the Lord did not come upon him until after he had obediently thrown down the altar of Baal that belonged to his father. (Judges 6:30-34) He had to be willing to destroy that altar, obeying God's will no matter what anyone else said or thought. There's a time and place to honor our parents, but God must come first. Since demonic activity is involved in idolatry, Gideon was taking spiritual authority over the strongholds that were oppressing him and his family.

Grinding our Idols to Powder

It's not enough to tear down our idols. If they're left intact, there's a tendency to go back and place them once again upon the altars of our hearts. So Josiah *"made dust of them."* He pulverized them beyond repair! Moses did the same thing with the golden calf. *"He took the calf which they had made, burned it in the fire, and ground it to powder."*

When Dagon, the idol of the Philistines, fell down the people simply put it back up on its stand the next morning. (1 Samuel 5:3) How many times have I seen believers (me included) tear down their idols one day, and then turn around and put them back up on the altar of their hearts the following day, week, or month! (Sometimes our idols are good things, even God-given blessings. We surely are not to grind those to powder! We are to make sure God is first, and then we are to take care of that which God gives to us as expressions of love and gratitude to Him.)

Desecrating the High Places

Josiah took things one step further. Not only did he tear down the idolatrous altars and make dust of them, but he also burned the bones of the unauthorized priests on them. Years before, an unnamed prophet said this would happen as he prophesied against Jeroboam's sinful altars:

> *O altar, altar! Thus says the Lord; Behold, a child, Josiah by name, shall be born to the house of David; and upon you he shall sacrifice the priests of the high places who burn incense on you, and men's bones shall be burned on you.*
>
> (1 Kings 13:2)

What was the purpose and significance of this? The bones desecrated those sinful altars and in doing so, it guaranteed that no one would dare come back to that place again. This symbolizes becoming so determined that we will not sin against our Lord that we voluntarily declare all places and forms of idolatry as forever off limits to us. It's called adamantly refusing to continue hurting God with our adulterous ways. This is truly having a heart after God and deeply repenting to the same degree that Joseph's brothers did in the book of Genesis, refusing to cause their father any more pain by their sinful actions:

> *And now, my lord, I cannot go back to my father without the boy [Benjamin]. Our father's life is bound up in the*

> *boy's life. So please, my lord, let me stay here as a slave instead of the boy, and let the boy return with his brothers. For how can I return to my father if the boy is not with me?* ***I couldn't bear to see the anguish this would cause my father!*** (Genesis 44:30, 33-34 NLT)

Judah decided he would rather be a slave for the rest of his life in a foreign country than to cause any more grief to his dear father. He couldn't bear to see any more anguish on his dad's face! That was it! They passed the test. They certainly had changed over the years, and for the better! Only then did Joseph revealed his identity to his repentant brothers. (Genesis 44:1-5) That reminds me of the day I decided to no longer bring any more anguish to the face of my earthly father when I was a teenager.

I wasn't aware the apartment complex near our home was one of the ones Dad was managing. I had some rowdy teenage friends who lived there and, unknown to my parents, I started drinking beer with them on the weekends. One day I went to their apartment and got very drunk with them. We were recklessly throwing things into the apartment community swimming pool which we shouldn't; stupidly thinking it was hilarious. Tenants soon called the office and Dad came out to chase us away, and wow, was he surprised to see me there. "Charles, get in the car. I'm taking you home," Dad sternly said. "In the backseat," he yelled as I went for the front passenger door. (Looking back, he probably wanted to protect me from being smacked with his angry fist.)

As we were halfway home, I finally sat up and looked up front into the car's rearview mirror. I had to scoot over a bit to "seek his face." I wanted to see how angry he was and perhaps then be able to guess how long I would be grounded for. There was no anger. Only anguish, disappointment, and deep, deep sadness. When we got home, he didn't pull off his belt to whip me like in times past. I wished he had. It would have been a lot less painful than watching his shoulders slump in utter defeat as he said through his tears, "I am in such shock over your actions that I don't know what to say. I'm so disappointed in you." He turned and slowly walked down the hallway to his bedroom in utter defeat.

He didn't live long enough to learn that that day was a major turning point in my life. I wouldn't get saved until years later, but at that point, I said in my heart, "I will never, ever so disappoint my father again." I no longer hung out with those wild friends. Dad didn't have to ground me. I grounded myself.

Years later, when I read God's promise to Solomon in 2 Chronicles 7:14, I remembered when I sought Dad's face in the car. Upon seeing the pain on his face, I turned from my wicked ways.

> *If My people who are called by My Name will humble themselves, and pray and seek My face, and turn from their wicked ways, then I will hear from heaven, and will forgive their sin and heal their land.*

There's a progression in this verse. We need to humble ourselves in order to be able to pray effectively, for God resists the proud, and knows them from afar off. (Psalm 38:6) As we fervently pray to the point that we are seeking His face, then the Lord will allow us to see His face, a face often grieved over our sins. Then He can put His finger upon those idols in our hearts that are wicked in His eyes, causing us—out of love for God—to turn away from them. This original promise was given to those who would find themselves under His chastening hand of drought or locusts or pestilence due to idolatry:

> *The Lord appeared to Solomon by night, and said to him: "I have heard your prayer, and have chosen this place for myself as a house of sacrifice. When I shut up heaven and there is no rain, or command the locusts to devour the land, or send pestilence among My people, if My people who are called by My Name will humble themselves, and pray and seek My face, and turn from their wicked ways, then I will hear from heaven, and will forgive their sin and heal their land."* (2 Chronicles 7:12-13)

In the Old Testament, the Lord shut up the heavens because of Ahab's idolatry, and sometimes allowed plagues and diseases (pandemics) to ravage the land. He allowed locusts to destroy their harvest so Joel's people would turn their wayward hearts back to Himself. Their wicked ways are clearly elaborated to Solomon in this same chapter.

> *If you turn away and forsake My statutes and My commandments which I have set before you, and go and serve other gods, and worship them, then I will uproot them from My land.* (2 Chronicles 7:19-20)

If we're going to be like David, we too will tear down and destroy our idols, and make sure we don't drift back to them, lest we grieve our Heavenly Father and our Lord Jesus. This type of determination is the result of a heart deeply in love.

Even with all his frailties, David was a man who lived way beyond his time, living like a Spirit-filled, New Testament believer in so many ways. He was blessed beyond measure, and even beyond his generation. His relationship with God is rarely equaled by believers, even today and we have so many more resources at our disposal, or are they distractions? When God called, David answered. When God stirred him, David responded and sought Him. When God loved him, David loved Him back:

> *When You said, "Seek My face," my heart said to You, "Your face, Lord, I will seek."* (Psalm 27:8)

David had a reciprocal relationship with his God. When God poured out love upon him, David, in response, poured out songs of worship and adoration and love to Him. Those kings who followed in David's footsteps are called revival Kings for they led God's people into repentance from idolatry, causing revival to come to their hearts and land. And yet, if we're not careful, even something as wonderful as revival can become an idol to us!

CHAPTER 15

The Idol of Revival?

"...that Your people may rejoice in You."
—Psalm 85:6

In the past few decades, I've enjoyed visiting places where God has poured out His Spirit in extraordinary ways. And yet, the Big Apple has not seen anything lately that resembles scriptural or historical revival. (We did have a taste of revival at Times Square Church in the early 1990's when people ran to the altars to get saved after David Wilkerson would conclude his anointed Sunday night evangelistic messages. We were baptizing dozens of new believers every single month for quite a while; for a couple of years.) But listen to the results of the revivalist Charles Finney's ministry upon Rochester, New York in 1831:

> Nearly all of the lawyers, judges, physicians, merchants, bankers and master mechanics of the city were among the converts; so that, according to unquestionable testimony, the whole character of the city was changed and has been famous ever since for its high moral tone, its strong churches, its evangelical and earnest ministry, and its frequent and powerful revivals of religion. Even the courts and prisons bore witness to its blessed effect. There was a wonderful falling off in crime. The courts had little to do, and the jail was nearly empty for years afterwards.[60]

I love to also read the amazing accounts of the first great awakening in our country under Jonathan Edward's ministry. Listen to the condition of his town of Northampton, Massachusetts in his own words, as they experienced what must be labeled as a spiritual awakening:

> There was scarcely a single person in the town, either old or young, that was left unconcerned about the great things of the eternal world. Souls did as it were come by flocks to Jesus Christ. The town seemed to be full of the Presence of God… Our young people, when they met, were wont [accustomed] to spend the time in talking of the excellency and dying love of Jesus Christ.[61]

For decades I've studied and prayed for revival for my mission field, New York City. So, I'll speak as one who desires to see what I've read about in the Word and in church history. A verse from the Psalms concerning revival touches on the essence of what I think a true awakening would entail:

> *Will You not revive us again, that Your people may rejoice in You?*
> (Psalm 85:6)

When we're truly scripturally revived, the focus of our hearts and lives will be squarely on the Lord, fellowshipping with Him, rejoicing in Him, worshipping Him, serving Him. Then we will corporately and individually be the witnesses that will draw the unsaved to Christ. Whether our nation repents to the level as described in 2 Chronicles 7:14 or not, you and I as individuals can choose to do so:

> *When He gives quietness, who then can make trouble? And when He hides His face, who then can see Him, whether it is against a nation or a man alone?* (Job 34:29)

While on staff with Michael Brown at FIRE School of Ministry, I recall him reflecting on his time as one of the leaders at the Pensacola Outpouring. He said,

> Revival services are like spiritual elevators. We certainly go to new levels, but we're not called to live in the elevator. We come out onto a new level of love for God and effectiveness as His on-fire witnesses.[62]

If revival becomes an all-consuming idol to us, we could be in danger of losing our discernment and then we'll accept anything that comes down the turnpike that's labeled a "revival." On the other side of the coin, and where the biggest danger is for most of us, if we're worshipping the idols of our religious traditions, we will probably exclude ourselves from any fresh moves of the Spirit of God. Phillip Brooks commented on this subject (in 1883!):

> In the best sense of the word, Jesus was a radical…His religion has been so long identified with conservatism—often with conservatism of the obstinate and unyielding sort—that it is almost startling for us sometimes to

> remember that all of the conservatism of His own times was against Him; that it was the young, free, restless, sanguine, progressive part of the people who flocked to Him.[63]

I long to see a revival like the one described in the book of Joel. The people of God turn to the Lord with all their hearts, responding to His call to do so:

> *Now, therefore, says the LORD, turn to Me with all your heart, with fasting, with weeping, and with mourning. So rend your heart, and not your garments; return to the LORD your God, for He is gracious and merciful, slow to anger, and of great kindness; and He relents from doing harm.* (Joel 2:12-13)

Turning wholeheartedly to the Lord includes being willing to rend (tear) our hearts away from anything that would try to take precedence over Him. Then we will not allow anything to hinder us from obediently coming to God and seeking His face:

> *Blow the trumpet in Zion, consecrate a fast, call a sacred assembly; gather the people, sanctify the congregation, assemble the elders, gather the children and nursing babes; let the bridegroom go out from his chamber, and the bride from her dressing room...* (Joel 2:15-16)

Nothing is more important than God; not family, not even wedding plans. As we start to know Him intimately, He becomes our shelter, our strength, and truly the Lord our God:

> *The LORD will be a shelter for His people, and the strength of the children of Israel. So you shall know that I am the LORD your God.* (Joel 3:16, 17)

If we become enamored with revival power or manifestations more than with Christ, we'll be placing our eyes upon temporary instead of eternal glory. And yet… there's something around the corner that's much more wonderful than any and all revivals: being the eternal bride of Christ! This is what we are destined for! This is the reality that God wants us to begin even now to embrace and walk in as we develop into people who become men and women after God's own heart, as a people and as individuals. The glorious, victorious end-time church will be filled with men and women who exclusively worship and adore our soon-coming Bridegroom-King. What an exciting time to be alive as bridal love will fill, satisfy, and transform those of us who wholeheartedly adore the Lord!

CHAPTER 16

Revelation: Is the Bride Ready Yet?

"The marriage of the Lamb has come, and His wife has made herself ready."
—Revelation 19:7

December 22nd will always be a special date on my calendar. It was the day my wife and I were married. I was an Associate Pastor at Times Square Church in Manhattan. The hand of God brought Lynn and me together and we were so excited about our "Christmas wedding." Every Christmas season a generous couple in the congregation would donate hundreds of red poinsettias and fill the stage with bright color and cheer. Since our wedding was three days before Christmas, the flowers were graciously ordered early enough to first be used for our wedding.

As Pastor Bob Phillips and I were waiting backstage, I looked out beyond those flowers to see that almost the whole lower level was filled with friends and family members. I was trying really hard not to get too nervous, so I struck up a conversation with Pastor Bob. He told me he had married hundreds of couples. What a relief that was! At least *he* wouldn't be nervous. He could do this in his sleep. As he noticed the crowd, he said something I didn't quite hear clearly. I thought he said, "This sure took a lot of sweat," referring to how the rest of the pastoral staff must have prayed extremely hard for God to bless me with such a lovely bride as Lynn.

"What did you say?" I replied with humorous amazement that he would make such a funny statement.

"I said, this is surely the biggest one yet," referring to the number of people present. He then continued, "It looks like everything's in place." He turned to one of the nearby ushers and asked, "Is the bride ready?"

"I… I don't know," the inexperienced usher stated.

"Well, we certainly can't start the service until we're sure the bride's ready! Can you go over to the front and find out for us?" Pastor Bob calmly asked.

"Uh, sure," the usher nervously replied as he rushed away. He came back about sixty seconds later, gasping for air and saying, "The bride… isn't quite… ready yet. She needs… a few more minutes."

A few moments later Lynn was being escorted down the aisle, smiling at me with the eyes of a bride who is totally and exclusively in love with her groom. Not only was her gown and veil in place, but also her heart was ready: ready to marry me! I could see it in her lovely eyes; eyes for me alone.

That important question that Pastor Bob asked, "Is the bride ready?" stuck with me because it reminded me of a conversation I had with Leonard Ravenhill a few years earlier. Brother Ravenhill was the author of many great books including the classic, *Why Revival Tarries.* But he was much more than a writer. He was a revivalist, a prayer warrior, and a modern-day prophet who was influential in the lives of those he mentored, especially David Wilkerson. He even was on staff at Brooklyn Teen Challenge as a teacher and preacher in the early years.

While I was on staff at the Times Square Church a few years earlier than the wedding, I jumped at the generous offer from Pastor Dave to take a vacation in Lindale, Texas where his World Challenge offices were located. The thought immediately entered and stayed in my mind, "I hope I have the opportunity to meet Leonard Ravenhill, since he lives in that same small town." Not only did I get to meet him, but he asked if I would like to come to his home and spend some time in prayer with him. He was very friendly and down to earth and we had a great time. After we finished praying as I was about to leave, I turned and asked him a question that had been on my heart for years:

"Brother Ravenhill, do you think America is going to experience one more revival before the coming of the Lord?"

Without any hesitation, he quickly replied, "Of course!" The expression on my face said, "But how can you be so sure?" so he continued. "It's about nine-thirty in the morning," he said as he glanced at his watch. "How many believers in this small town do you think prayed before going to work today?" I shrugged my shoulders, signifying not very many. "How many of them," he continued, "spent more than a few minutes with the Lord?"

"Probably not very many," I answered.

Then he said, "Does that sound to you like His bride has made herself ready…for the marriage of the Lamb?" I knew what passage he was referring to.

> *Let us be glad and rejoice and give Him glory, for the marriage of the Lamb has come, and His wife has made herself ready.* (Revelation 19:7)

What Brother Ravenhill said gave me great hope and encouragement. I realized the bride upon the earth surely is not ready, but God in His grace will get us ready. Before we get raptured into heaven (whenever that will be), our hearts will first be enraptured with our Groom. Brother Ravenhill was viewing life through the prophetic paradigm of spousal faithfulness. The Lord's wife, the bride of Christ, will be ready for the eternal wedding, *"a bride beautifully dressed for her husband."* (Revelation 21:2 NLT) Lynn was ready to marry me and I was ready to marry her, over thirty years ago!

Jesus, our Bridegroom God, enables us to forsake all others, including ourselves… for Him! He expects this from us. One day Jesus turned to the crowd and said,

> *He who loves father or mother more than Me is not worthy of Me. And he who loves son or daughter more than Me is not worthy of Me. And he who does not take his cross and follow after Me is not worthy of Me.* (Matthew 10:37-38)

"Not worthy of" means to not be fit, suitable, or the same as. The Greek word pictures a scale that balances two equal sides, measuring the same exact weight. Jesus is declaring, "If you don't love Me supremely, you don't love Me the way I love you." Eve was a worthy and suitable companion for Adam, bone of his bones and flesh of his flesh. The Bible teaches us that if we love something or someone else more than we love the Lord, that makes us more like a harlot than a bride. Jesus doesn't want to marry a bride who is a gold digger, one who is just out for His possessions. He wants us to love Him as much as He loves us. He has set his heart upon winning our hearts. He's coming back for a faithful bride, a ready bride. This Groom is determined to win our undivided love. The Lord is still (under the New Covenant) sending out His prophets to seek His wandering sheep and His wandering bride.

Are we faithful to and intimate with Jesus, or are we often unfaithful and aloof towards Him? Are we more concerned about understanding prophetic passages than in listening to the Lord's messages to the wayward churches in Revelation? The Lord is still saying to us,

> *Anyone with ears to hear must listen to the Spirit and understand what He is saying to the churches... I correct and discipline everyone I love. So be diligent and turn from your indifference. Look! I stand at the door and knock. If you hear my voice and open the door, I will come in, and we will share a meal together as friends.*
>
> (Revelation 3:13, 19, 20 NLT)

The Lord ministered deeply to me in a hard season when I thought I was a total failure. He told me how much He individually loves me. But even more needful—and helpful—was His correction as He revealed His absolute faithfulness to me, exposing my unfaithful heart towards Him. I then learned (through the Scriptures) that idolatry in the lives of those who are in a covenant relationship with God is equivalent to spiritual adultery, which provokes Him to jealousy.

Honestly, I was initially ashamed of the indifference I had over how I nonchalantly mistreated the Lord. How often we mistreat Jesus Christ! We neglect, ignore, and do not appreciate Him as we should. We often treat acquaintances and friends better than Him. As our heavenly Husband, He has given and given and given to us, not so He could receive back from us; but it surely grieves Him when we do not deeply love Him in return. And yet, He continues to love and pursue us. There's no one like Jesus!

Bridal Love is Exclusive

Repentance over our spiritual adultery leads to a reviving and blossoming of our "first love" into an even deeper "bridal love" characterized by exclusive worship. On the day that my wife and I were married, it was her eyes that totally captivated me. We have many beautiful photographs of our wedding day, but one picture stands out as the groom's favorite. It's the one where my wife is making her vows to me, lovingly gazing into my eyes with that look of a faithful bride. I knew then (and I still know today) that she has eyes only for me. It was her doves' eyes that were the most beautiful thing of that ceremony, the most beautiful thing I've ever seen! Listen to the Groom in the Song of Solomon:

> *You are beautiful, my darling,* ***beautiful beyond words. Your eyes are like doves*** *behind your veil... You have captured my heart, my treasure, my bride. You hold it hostage with one glance of your eyes.*
>
> (Song of Solomon 4:1, 9 NLT)

What does having "doves' eyes" refer to? Matthew Henry's comments on this verse are:

> Thou hast doves' eyes, clear and chaste, and often cast up toward heaven…When our aims and intentions are sincere and honest, then we have doves' eyes, when we look not unto idols but have our eyes ever toward the Lord.[64]

The most beautiful adornment a bride can have is not her veil or even her white gown, but dove's eyes! When a bride leaves her family and her singleness behind and gives herself wholeheartedly to her husband, it's the type of commitment the Lord is looking for in His bride. This is the beauty spoken of regarding the Queen (for King Jesus in Psalm 45):

> *Listen, O daughter, consider and incline your ear; forget your own people also, and your father's house;* ***so the King will greatly desire your beauty;*** *because He is your* *Lord, worship Him.* (vs. 10, 11)

Many marriages (even among Christians) never enjoy the depth of unity, love, and blessing that God has made available because one partner is giving and loving and extending themselves while the other is just a taker. They take and take without ever thinking about the selfishness of their ways. That's the way much of the bride of Christ is today towards Him. How many of us are deeply concerned with how Jesus feels? How many truly enjoy just bringing joy to the heart of God? May the lovers of Jesus arise in this generation! We seek revival, blessings, and prosperity. We seek His hands, but are we seeking His face? As the bride of Christ, are we the type of people who pursue a husband just for His wealth, or for Him?

After many years of marriage, I'm glad to say that my wife Lynn still has those doves' eyes, eyes only for me. But this is not true of every bride. The sad fact is that every single adulterous spouse was once a beautiful bride or groom. No one decides in the beginning of their marriage to one day commit adultery on their beloved spouse. The process can begin very slowly and unnoticeably. Perhaps a mate is ignored or neglected and they drift towards someone who comes along to meet their unfulfilled emotional needs. Many who have committed adultery have admitted it wasn't primarily a physical thing at first. It began when they looked to another to meet their needs.

The same principle is true concerning committing spiritual adultery against our God. Jeroboam didn't really worship those lifeless golden calves he set up. He was simply looking to his own wisdom instead of relying on the Lord to guard the blessings that God Himself had given him. Some of the kings of Israel married foreign wives as part of strategic, political alliances with surrounding nations. Their root problem was they were not looking to the Lord as the source of their security.

The people who worshipped King Herod in the book of Acts did so because they were depending too heavily on his governmental assistance to meet their earthly needs. (Acts 12:20) Ministers who compromise their convictions to protect their positions or pensions are sometimes doing so because they're not looking to the Lord as their ultimate source of income and security. We must also follow David's example of total dependency on the Lord, or we could unintentionally drift into the arms of another god. David declared,

> *To You, O Lord, I lift up my soul. O my God, I trust in You...* ***My eyes are ever toward the Lord,*** *for He shall*

> *pluck my feet out of the net... Our eyes look to the* Lord *our God, until He has mercy on us.* (Psalm 25:1, *15; 123:2)*

Why look to dried up wells when we can go to the water fountain that never runs dry? (Jeremiah 2:13) Who needs foreign wives for security? Who needs golden calves to protect their lot in life? Not me! I, like David, will therefore look to the Lord *"from whence cometh my help."* (Psalm 121:1 KJV)

I'm on a journey with the Lord to the land of faithfulness, where His utter faithfulness to me is helping me to become sincerely and consistently faithful to Him. What about you, beloved? God is in an amazing and wonderful process of bringing His people into the realities described in the book of Revelation.[65] Paul's description of "a glorious church, not having spot or wrinkle" will surely come to pass! (Eph. 5:27)

CHAPTER 17

Abominations Always Cause Desolation

"A deceived heart has turned him aside."
—Isaiah 44:20

Reading the Book of Revelation is like watching two movies on one screen at the same time! On the top half of the screen is a spiritual movie, filled with angels and heavenly things; and the lower screen is filled with earthly and demonic scenes. It begins with John on a prison island, and yet he is *"in the Spirit on the Lord's Day."* The prophetic trumpet voice of Jesus—our New High Priest—dictates seven letters for the seven churches in Asia Minor, and then John is invited into the Throne Room in Heaven. The future unfolds before him (and us) as the seven sealed scrolls are opened. As heaven prepares for a wedding, Earth is preparing for war. As we're invited to worship the

Lamb, Earth worships a man whose number is 666. And in the midst of all this, we find two women battling for the souls of mankind: a consecrated bride and a great harlot.

> G. R. Beasley-Murray writes, The Revelation as a whole may be characterized as *A Tale of Two Cities*, with the subtitle, *The Harlot and the Bride*... The harlot-city reposes on the beast from hell—she partakes of the character of the devil, and the bride-city descends from heaven–she is the creation of God. But one thing they have in common. They stand alike on the earth and invite humanity to come to them.
>
> Jeremiah Johnson adds, In the last days, there will be two dueling brides that will emerge—the Consecrated Bride and the Harlot Bride. The Consecrated Bride will marry itself to the Bridegroom King, the Man of War, and the Harlot Bride will marry itself to the world.[66]

We focused in the last chapter on the bride who prepares to marry the Lamb, but we also need to see that a harlot will draw multitudes into worshipping a Beast-man, a.k.a. the Antichrist, the Instead-of-Christ. This corrupt worship will prove fatal to all who partake of it:

> ***If anyone worships the beast and his image*** *and receives a mark on his forehead or on his hand, he shall also drink the wine of God's fury, poured full strength into the cup of His wrath.* (Revelation 14:9)

It's interesting to note how Jesus described this:

> *"When you see* ***the 'abomination of desolation,'*** *spoken of by Daniel the prophet, standing in the holy place" (whoever*

> *reads, let him understand), "then let those who are in Judea flee to the mountains."* (Matthew 24:14-15)

I believe this speaks of the idol worship the Roman General Titus brought with him into Jerusalem in 70 AD *and* the future idol worship of the Beast and his miraculous statue described in Revelation:

> *He was granted power to give breath to the image of the beast, that the image of the beast should both speak and cause as many as would not worship the image of the beast to be killed.* (13:15)

It appears that the greatest sign this false prophet will perform is the making of a statue of this Antichrist which will then be supernaturally and demonically empowered to speak... declaring that those who do not worship the image of the beast are to be killed. It's not just the mark of the Beast that will prove to be fatal. It's the worship of the Beast and his statue that destroys people. This statue is the Abomination of Desolation, that is, the abominable idol which causes total desolation to its worshippers. Those who worship it will be forever damned because the desolation done to them completely destroys their ability to discern what is true and what is a lie.

Idolatry Always Destroys Discernment

Although this particular "Abomination" will cause complete, irreversible "Desolation," the truth is, every single idol that we worship causes spiritual desolation to us to one degree or another. I would not be faithful to the scriptural view of idolatry if I neglected to share how dangerous and destructive idolatry is. Idolatry opens people up to powerful deception through a loss of discernment. Isaiah describes the utter foolishness of a man who cuts down a tree to use one part of it for firewood and another part to make a wooden idol god:

> *None considers in his heart, neither is there knowledge nor understanding to say, "I have burned part of it in the fire; yea, also I have baked bread upon the coals thereof; I have roasted flesh, and eaten it: and shall I fall down to the stock of a tree?"* ***A deceived heart has turned him aside, that he cannot deliver his soul, nor say, "Is there not a lie in my right hand?"*** (Isaiah 44:19-20)

This is in fulfillment of the built-in judgment the Psalmist declared will follow all those who make or worship idols:

> *(The heathen's) idols are silver and gold, the works of men's hands. They have mouths, but they speak not: eyes have they, but they see not: they have ears, but they hear not: noses have they, but they smell not.* ***They that make them are like unto them; so is every one that trusts in them.***
> (Psalm 115:6-7)

Those who make, worship, or trust in idols become as blind and deaf as the things they worship. That explains why some people in cults become so deceived, falling into strange and false teachings. As they worship their leader instead of worshipping the one true Master, Jesus Christ, they begin to lose their discernment. Idols are veils over the hearts of people, causing them to not be able to behold the glory of God or the truths in the Bible.

When we disobey the first commandment by making something more important to us than God, that thing between us and God—that idol—becomes a veil over the eyes of our hearts. A heart that indulges in idolatry becomes a deceived heart that turns aside from the truth and cannot discern properly. Satan knows this and will use these truths to bring total desolation to those who fall into the idolatry that will come in the very last days, as seen in Revelation.

Other Warnings Regarding Idolatry

The scriptural warnings against idolatry in the New Testament are numerous and frightful. For instance:

> *Do you not know that the unrighteous will not inherit the kingdom of God? Do not be deceived. Neither fornicators,* ***nor idolaters,*** *nor adulterers, nor homosexuals, nor sodomites, nor thieves, nor covetous, nor drunkards, nor revilers, nor extortioners* ***will inherit the kingdom of God.*** (1 Corinthians 6:9-10)

Those who repent after falling into the act of adultery, fornication, idolatry, or homosexuality will find a loving and forgiving God ready to restore them back to fellowship with Him and His people. But if one moves in with their sin-partner, they are in danger of embracing that sinful relationship to the point they could be classified as becoming a fornicator, an adulterer, or a homosexual… and those who persist in those sinful lifestyle choices will not inherit the kingdom of God.

During a counseling session, a church leader told me that he decided to leave his wife and kids and move in with his "hot" secretary because, he said, "I'd rather enjoy sex with her for the next few years than to stay with my boring wife." How should I have counseled him? I gently but firmly explained that adultery is certainly forgivable, but choosing to move in with her and becoming an adulterer will put his eternal soul in jeopardy.

He looked right at me and replied, "I'd rather keep my sexy mistress and take my chances." He abruptly got up and left the room. I hope he has since repented.

> Psalm 73 says, "*For indeed, those who are far from You shall perish; You have destroyed all those who desert You for harlotry. But it is good for me to draw near to God; I have put my trust in the* Lord *God, that I may declare all Your works.*" (27-28)

Let's not desert the Lord for harlotry. Instead, let's draw near to God, repent of our idolatry, put our trust in Him, and declare all His works!

CHAPTER 18

The Remedy to Idolatry is Adoration

"We adore You as the One who is over all things."
1 Chronicles 29:11 NLT

As the end draws near and things look bleaker and darker, we turn to the Scriptures and we don't see a defeated, end time church. But instead, we read about an adoring bride, eagerly ready to marry her Bridegroom. Yes, in the book of Revelation, as the sorrows of Earth begin to fade away and the glories of New Jerusalem come into focus, we hear God's people crying out the universal word of worship and praise: *"Hallelujah!"*

> *I heard what sounded like a great multitude, like the roar of rushing waters and like loud peals of thunder, shouting:*

> *"Hallelujah! For our Lord God Almighty reigns."*
> (Revelation 19:6 NIV)

Do you know what the word "hallelujah" means? Probably more than you've previously realized. In Strong's Greek Dictionary of the New Testament we find its full definition: *"Praise ye Jah, an exclamation of adoration."*[67] Nave's Topical Bible definition is similar: *"Hallelujah, an exclamatory expression of praise or adoration."*[68] Clearly the word hallelujah entails more than just praise, and even more than worship. It includes adoration. Adoration is defined as: "Deep love and respect; worship."[69] It is a type of heartfelt worship to God in which we express our love for Him and to Him. A.W. Tozer said that adoration is:

> To love God with all the power within us. To love God with fear and wonder and yearning and awe.[70]
>
> Tozer also wrote: It is simply not enough to know about God. We must know God in increasing levels of intimacy that lifts us up above all reason and into the world of adoration and praise and worship.[71]
>
> Eric Gilmour adds: Many people go into the closet to pray and they leave the same way that they came in, simply because they did everything but adore Him. Adoration is the beginning, the sustaining, and the end of all things in God. Anyone can pray, but God looks for those who will let go of everything else and adore Him. He thirsts for those who only want Him.[72]

Since our God gets overwhelmingly jealous over our misdirected worship, surely He gets overwhelmingly joyful when we finally worship Him exclusively. Just as reading E.M.

Bounds's classic books on prayer often cause me to put them down and pray, and Leonard Ravenhill's writings drive me to stop and repent, it would be great if any time during your reading of this chapter, you put it down and spend time in worship and adoration of our God!

Adoration is the response of love from a heart that has been first loved and captivated by God. This is worshipping God in spirit and in truth. This is what Our Father is looking for. Jesus said,

> *Your worship must engage your spirit in the pursuit of truth. That's the kind of people the Father is out looking for... Those who worship him must do it out of their very being, their spirits, their true selves, in adoration.*
>
> (John 4:23-24 MSG)

Proverbs 15:8b teaches us that, "*The prayer of the upright is His delight.*" Since God delights in our prayers to Him, how much more does He delight in our adoration of Him! David knew that God delighted in him, and he knew that his praise and worship and adoration truly blessed the heart of his God.

> *O Lord, the God of our ancestor Israel, may you be praised forever and ever! Yours, O Lord, is the greatness, the power, the glory, the victory, and the majesty. We adore you as the One who is over all things.*
>
> (1 Chronicles 29:10-11 NLT)

As we develop a life of worship and adoration, something deeply profound clicks into place within our spirits. A few anonymous quotes bear witness to this:

- "Adoring Christ is the highest form of worship."

- "Adore the Lord Jesus Christ, and your life will never be the same."
- "In adoring Christ, we discover ourselves; we find our purpose and the true meaning of life."

As we adore Him, we begin to touch upon and flow into the eternal intention for which we have been made. God's eternal purpose, the plan of redemption, centers around the marriage of His Son to His bride, the church. It's our pure, sanctified worship and adoration that now and forever will be the way we express our love to Him. We're not just called out of all types of idolatry, but called into fervent and pure adoration of our Savior:

> Fiery love for Jesus pushes our thoughts out of hiding and puts them into anointed words of adoration.[73]
>
> —Brian Simmons

Our worship is pure when it is exclusive, adoring Him alone, as Augustine said, *"Christ is not valued at all unless He be valued above all."*

> Raymond Ortlund agrees: The gospel reveals that, as we look out into the universe, ultimate reality is not cold, dark, blank space; ultimate reality is romance. There is a God above with love in His eyes for us and infinite joy to offer us, and He has set Himself upon winning our hearts for Himself alone… More than our popular churches and institutions and movements, God wants us ourselves. He wants our hearts, our loyalty, our love for Himself alone.[74]

Adoration is what must fill our emptied hearts once we have turned away from all our outward and inward idols.

It is the remedy that will keep our hearts from wandering. We do not want to be empty, swept, and garnished (like the Pharisees), and then become susceptible to the next idol we run across, especially those pesky idols of self: self-righteousness, self-exaltation, self-centeredness. Adoration is learned through practice, similar to learning to swim or ride a bicycle. I can tell you all about it, but you must learn through personally adoring your God for yourself.

I once opened up my School of Ministry class for whatever questions the students would like to ask me. A young man quickly raise his hand and asked, "Pastor Charles, if you could go back and start your ministry life all over again with the knowledge, experience, and wisdom that you have now, what would you do differently? I answered with no hesitation. "I would spend much more time worshiping and adoring my Lord." And since we're never too old to learn, I'm determined to spend more time in adoration. I encourage you to add that ingredient to your devotional life. Add songs of adoration, prayers of adoration, and proclamations of adoration to God. When I wake up in the morning, every morning, I kiss my wife and tell her that I love her. I tell her the same when we go to sleep, and if we're both off work, then throughout the day, as well. And adoration is one of the best ways to express our love to Jesus. We could say that Jesus' love languages are three-fold. He receives love from us through our obedience, our love for His people, and our adoration of Him.

> John 14:21—*He who has My commandments and keeps them, it is he who loves Me.*

> 1 John 4:20-21—*If someone says, "I love God," and hates his brother, he is a liar; for he who does not love his brother*

whom he has seen, how can he love God whom he has not seen? And this commandment we have from Him: that he who loves God must love his brother also.

How have I overcome (and remain free from) idolatry? I have accepted what the Scriptures teach about idolatry and spiritual adultery. I have repented of my idolatry, and am learning how to fill my life with adoration to Christ. Here's a few more quotes I have found helpful:

> Adoration is the spontaneous yearning of the heart to worship, honor, magnify, and bless God. We ask nothing but to cherish Him. We seek nothing but His exaltation. We focus on nothing but His goodness.[75]
>
> —Richard J. Foster

> The life of true holiness is rooted in the soil of awed adoration.[76] —J. I. Packer

> Worship is the actual act of ascribing worth directly to God. Worshipful actions may do this indirectly, but when the Bible commands and commends worship as our highest expression, it is not talking about anything other than direct, intentional, vertical outpourings of adoration.[77] —James MacDonald

> Brothers and Sisters, the very best work which we ever do on earth is to adore. You are blessed in prayer, but you are seven times blessed in praise![78]
>
> —Charles Spurgeon

Beloved, we are destined to become a glorious, holy, adoring church. We will be as in love with Jesus as He is with us, and as faithful to Him as He has always been and always will be to us!

Raymond Ortlund wrote,

> The biblical theme of spiritual harlotry is not the whole of theology. It is only one strand woven into the fabric of Scripture, along with others, all of which are needed for the whole tapestry to shine forth in its complexity and fullness. But this strand of God's marital love and of his people's presently harlotrous but ultimately faithful response is too much neglected. And it is the overlooked themes of Scripture to which any given age of the church must pay special attention, for it is precisely there that we most urgently need to hear the Word of God again.[79]

It's taken me a long time and much soul-searching (and God-searching) to get to the point that I can say, by the grace of God, idolatry does not dominate my life any longer. I have intentionally allowed adoration to dominate my life instead! I can liken my roller-coaster spiritual journey to the recorded history of the children of Israel.

Israel's Journey and Our Journey

Just as Paul (in 1st Corinthians, Chapter 10) paralleled our walk with Christ with Israel's wilderness journey, we can match particular books of the Bible with various stages in our Christian walk. So, where in the Bible are you? In Genesis, Exodus, Joshua, the Prophets, or perhaps Ezra; or maybe the Gospels or even James?

GENESIS, the book of beginnings, parallels the truth that we all began our journey lost and enslaved to this world.

EXODUS represents salvation, being delivered from Pharaoh and sin.

In **NUMBERS** we begin our wilderness wanderings as God performs miracle after miracle for us.

JOSHUA wins victories through God's power, and we do the same as we are established in God's Word and in His church—coming into a Land of Promise flowing with milk and honey.

JUDGES is where the people of God turn away from Him, become oppressed by foreign invasions, and cry out to Him for help. He raised up judges to deliver them only to have this cycle repeat over and over again.

In **SAMUEL, KINGS, AND CHRONICLES** they worshiped the false gods of heathen nations, similar to believers who, having lost their first love, begin to look to other things for their security, their happiness, and/or their identity.

JEREMIAH, HOSEA, AND THE OTHER PRE-EXILE PROPHETIC BOOKS represent those who are not responding to God's call to repentance and to return to our first love.

EZEKIEL represents those whom God has allowed to enter chastening captivities.

EZRA parallels the believer who is beginning to mourn over their unfaithfulness to the Lord, realizing how quickly and how easily we return to idolatry.

And then we came to **ZECHARIAH** which outlines Israel's (and our) total deliverance from idolatry through beholding the Lamb who was slain, pierced in the very heart by our sins.

In **THE GOSPELS** John the Baptist was called to confront the religious Jews of his day who forsook outward idolatry only to take up the dangerous inner worship of self; admiring how outwardly righteous they were.

In **JAMES** we see that the message of spiritual adultery is also for individual believers under the New Covenant.

REVELATION is our destiny as God's Word concludes with a Bride and Groom living happily ever after!

I came out of Egypt (the world) and although was greatly blessed in the Promised Land (the Christian Life), I soon found my heart going after so many other things. I experienced various Babylonian captivities, and yet, afterwards would go right back into worldly pursuits which inevitably led me right back into idolatry. When the prophetic message of God's jealousy over my idols first came to me, I received it enough to make sure I became outwardly clean (empty, swept, and garnished), and I was very proud of my lack of worldly contaminations. Since the idols of self were not exposed and dethroned yet, my life wavered between self-righteousness and self-condemnation, according to how I felt "I" was doing.

And then I realized how deeply my idolatry pierces and crushes God's heart, and I began to seek Him for the remedy to not go back into those things that provoke His holy jealousy. The revelation of His deep love for me awakened a desire that I would be faithful to Him like He's faithful to me, that I would love Him like He loves me, and that I would express my love to Him like He daily expresses His love to me. I then realized the answer was on my very lips all along. Hallelujah! Not just, "Hallelujah, praise the Lord," but "Hallelujah, praise ye Jah, and exclamation of adoration."

As I'm daily pouring the costly and fragrant oil of adoration onto the feet of my King, expressing my love for Him to Him, my heart has found my Home, my soul has found my Beloved, and my mind is beginning to realize just how much the Lord Jesus Christ enjoys receiving my adoration of Him! I wonder just how deeply I can fall in love with this amazing Bridegroom King! I'm determined to find out. Yes, Revelation concluding with Jesus and His Bride living happily ever after in a place filled with thunderous adoration. Raymond Ortlund wrote,

> The New Testament elevates human marriage to the place of mirroring Christ and the church in a holy, loving covenant, destined to live together forever. They shall live happily ever after, fulfilling every fairy tale and romance story ever written.[80]

The church then will have overcome her last hurdle, spiritual adultery; and thereafter there will be no idols in heaven! Oh Lord, make our hearts like heaven.

CHAPTER 19

Overflowing with Confident Hope

"I pray that God, the source of hope,
will fill you completely with joy and peace because
you trust in him. Then you will overflow
with confident hope through the power of the Holy Spirit."
—Romans 15:13 NLT

The last sermon I preached at Times Square Church was from the prophetic book of Hosea, paralleling his dealings with his wayward wife to the waywardness of Israel, and the waywardness of you and me, today. Pastor Dave stayed around that evening until there were only a handful of people left in the Mark Hellinger Theater.

"Come, walk with me to my apartment, Charles," he said.

As we made our way out the back door and down 51st Street towards Eighth Avenue, he wasted no time. "That was a great message tonight. And I could tell you put a lot of study and prayer behind it."

"Thank you," I simply replied.

Near the front entrance to the Worldwide Plaza, he abruptly stopped and turned to me. "But let me tell you how you could have made it even better. No matter how hard the messages of the prophets were, they ended with hope: Jeremiah's promises in chapters 29 and 30; Ezekiel chapter 47 with waters to swim in; Isaiah with the triumphant Messianic Kingdom. And the same with the book of Hosea. Next time you preach from it, spend time sharing about the victory and restoration that's found in its last chapter."

I couldn't wait to get home that evening and pull out my Bible and read that last chapter of Hosea. Here we see Israel finally forsaking all her idols and becoming faithful and totally dependent on the living God, instead of looking to alliances with sinful nations.

> *O Israel, return to the* L*ORD your God, for you have stumbled because of your iniquity; take words with you, and return to the Lord. Say to Him, "Take away all iniquity; receive us graciously, for we will offer the sacrifices of our lips. Assyria shall not save us… nor will we say anymore to the work of our hands, 'You are our gods.' For in You the fatherless finds mercy."* (Hosea 14:1-2)

God's response is wonderful:

> *"I will heal their backsliding; I will love them freely, for My anger has turned away from him." Ephraim shall say,*

> ***"What have I to do anymore with idols? I have heard and observed Him." "I am like a green cypress tree; your fruit is found in Me."*** (Hosea 14:3, 8)

As we also observe the Lord and see Him as He is, we behold the One who is like a cypress or evergreen tree, consistently and forever faithful, giving us all the fruit we need, always green and always full of life and love and mercy. When we see Christ as He is, we have no need for any dumb idols to meet any of our needs. Amen? Then will come to pass the promises from Hosea, chapter 2:

> *I will wipe the many names of Baal from your lips, and you will never mention them again. I will make you my wife forever, showing you righteousness and justice, unfailing love and compassion. I will be faithful to you and make you mine, and you will finally know me as the LORD... I will say, "Now you are my people." And they will reply, "You are our God!"*

We mentioned earlier God's call to rend our hearts away from idolatry (from the prophetic book of Joel) until our main focus in life is God Himself. Look at God's hope-filled promises given to those who do so:

> *Be glad then, you children of Zion, and rejoice in the LORD your God; for He has given you the former rain faithfully, and He will cause the rain to come down for you—**the former rain, and the latter rain in the first month...** And it shall come to pass afterward that I will pour out My Spirit on all flesh; your sons and your daughters shall prophesy, your old men shall dream dreams, your young men shall see visions. And also on My menservants and on*

My maidservants I will pour out My Spirit in those days.
(Joel 2:23, 28, 29)

Regarding these former and latter rains:

> After planting, a seasonal rain provided moisture for germination and initial growth. This was called the "early [or former] rain." Later, near the time for harvest, another watering was referred to as the "latter rain." So, while the first rain was important for germination, the second rain provided nourishment that was important for the harvest." (From Bible Ask)[81]

Peter explained the supernatural events on the Day of Pentecost in Acts 2 as the fulfillment of Joel's prophecy of the outpouring of the Holy Spirit. Many Bible scholars believe Joel's famous "outpouring of the Spirit" prophecy speaks of the early outpouring when the church was birthed in Acts and the final outpouring which will prepare the final harvest of souls right before Christ returns. Surely, the final outpouring must fulfill all that is promised in Joel's prophecy. I'm referring to this part: "*Your young men shall see visions, your old men shall dream dreams.*"

We have interpreted these verses as saying that visions and dreams are parts of the Spirit-filled life that we can expect to experience today, along with the gift of prophecy: "*...and they shall prophesy*" (v. 18). And that is a correct interpretation, that God will pour out His Spirit generously upon everyone in these last days (everyone who is thirsty), men and women, sons and daughters, young and old alike. But there's more that is being declared and promised to us here. The key to unlocking this is to realize that dreams and visions are the expressed means by which God communicates with His prophets:

> Numbers 12:6: *Then He [God] said, "Hear now My words: If there is a prophet among you, I, the LORD, make Myself known to him in a vision; I speak to him in a dream."*

God clearly tells us here how He communicates with His prophets—through visions and dreams. So, the last days outpouring will not just enable us all to flow in spiritual gifts, but it will also give us, young and old, men and women alike a prophet's perspective on life, the world, and most importantly, the very heart of God Himself. God is promising here to reveal His heart to all of us, just as He did to His prophets of old. Moses longed for that day to come. We see this longing when he rebuked Joshua for trying to stop some tardy elders from prophesying:

> *Moses... gathered the seventy men of the elders of the people and placed them around the tabernacle. Then the LORD came down in the cloud, and spoke to him, and took of the Spirit that was upon him, and placed the same upon the seventy elders; and it happened, when the Spirit rested upon them, that they prophesied, although they never did so again. But two men had remained in the camp... and the Spirit rested upon them [and] they prophesied. And a young man ran and told Moses, and said, "Eldad and Medad are prophesying in the camp." So Joshua the son of Nun, Moses' assistant answered and said, "Moses my lord, forbid them!" Then Moses said to him, "Are you zealous for my sake?* ***Oh, that all the LORD's people were prophets and that the LORD would put His Spirit upon them!"***

That day is dawning upon us, a final outpouring of His Spirit which will bring us all into the realm of the prophets. The five-fold ministers will work themselves out of their jobs:

> *Now these are the gifts Christ gave to the church: the apostles, the prophets, the evangelists, and the pastors and teachers. Their responsibility is to equip God's people to do his work and build up the church, the body of Christ. This will continue until we all come to such unity in our faith and knowledge of God's Son that we will be mature in the Lord, measuring up to the full and complete standard of Christ.* (Ephesians 4:11-13 NLT)

The prophets (aka seers, 1 Samuel 9:9) not only see things in the spirit realm, but more importantly, they see and know the broken heart of God and His jealousy caused by our idolatry. David Wilkerson, a modern-day prophet, was adamantly against being placed on pedestals for at least two reasons. First of all, he knew it was unhealthy for people to think of him more highly than they ought to. (See 2 Corinthians 12:6) He knew he was just a man. And secondly, he knew we Christians like to make excuses for our lukewarmness. Instead of being convicted by his example, it's easier to say that he was a special breed of believer. That gets us off the hook. Instead of a special breed, he was a forerunner, a type of End Time believer who was completely in love with Christ. Although… "*Elijah was a human being, even as we are… he prayed earnestly…*" (James 5:17) And so did Pastor Dave. He once told me,

> "I don't like it when people put me up on a pedestal. I'm not special; I'm just diligent. They want to label me as special in order to justify their lack of zeal for God."

To the Last Days Church God desires to communicate His heart to us just as He did and does to His prophets. It's a heart burning with jealousy, a redeeming, transforming jealousy within the heart of El Kanna, our Jealous God. It's through knowing Him that we will love Him deeply and adore Him forever.

Quoting from my book, *Walking in the Footsteps of David Wilkerson:*

> I saw a man who not only carried the burden of God, but was deeply impacted by it. That was David's tenderness. He was thinking and feeling with God's heart. David Wilkerson knew that the touch of God is available to every hungry believer, and he longed for the day when an outpouring of God's Spirit would cause a whole generation of giant-killing believers to be raised up. Who will reach the unsaved Nicky Cruzes of our generation? Who is hungry for an outpouring that turns us into people carrying a prophet's revelation of the majesty, heart, and pain of God?[82]

John, the Beloved Apostle, simply concluded: *"Little children, keep yourselves from idols. Amen."* (1 John 5:20-21) The Amplified Bible says:

> *Little children, keep yourselves from idols (false gods)—[from anything and everything that would occupy the place in your heart due to God, from any sort of substitute for Him that would take first place in your life].*

Closing Prayer: Heavenly Father, thank you for the reader who has journeyed with me through the prophetic view of Your jealousy over our idols. By Your amazing grace, enable us to face and come out of our idolatry, our self-centeredness, and our lukewarmness and be prepared to meet our Bridegroom, adorned with a heart after God that exclusively, wholeheartedly, and extravagantly adores our Groom! If Christ delays

His coming, may we now in our day be filled with the type of bridal love for Him that He deserves. In Jesus' Name. Amen and Hallelujah!

O COME, LET US ADORE HIM

O come, let us adore Him,
O come, let us adore Him,
O come, let us adore Him,
Christ the Lord.

For He alone is worthy,
For He alone is worthy,
For He alone is worthy,
Christ the Lord.

Let's praise His name together,
Let's praise His name together,
Let's praise His name together,
Christ the Lord.

We'll give Him all the glory,
We'll give Him all the glory,
We'll give Him all the glory,
Christ the Lord.[84]

Idols Mentioned in this Book:

About the Author

Charles Simpson was raised in Tennessee. As a teenager, he received a missionary call to New York City where he has spent most of his adult life, pastoring, planting churches, and working in Bible schools. While serving as the pastor of prayer at Times Square Church, he married his wife, Lynn. They have worked alongside great leaders such as David and Don Wilkerson, Michael Brown, Peter Wagner, Brian Simmons, Joel Sadaphal, Russell Hodgins, Will Kitchen, Garry Patrylo, and Paul Burke. Pastor Charles served as the campus pastor at Brooklyn Teen Challenge and is planting his 5th church in Queens (www.oasislic.com).

Other Titles by Charles Simpson:

Walking in the Footsteps of David Wilkerson,
The Journey and Reflections of a Spiritual Son

Christian Island:
Parables About Pride, Gossip, and Discontentment

Angel Lucifer, Evil's Origin:
A Theological Novel

John: The Gospel of Sonship:
Learning to Abide in the Bosom of the Father

The Bosom of the Father:
The Place Jesus Has Prepared For Us

Endnotes

1 Daniel 6:26 - I make a decree that in every dominion of my kingdom men must tremble and fear before the God of Daniel. For He is the living God, and steadfast forever; His kingdom is the one which shall not be destroyed, and His dominion shall endure to the end.

2 *Assemblies of God Statement of Fundamental Truths*, https://ag.org/beliefs/statement-of-fundamental-truths #2

3 Terence E. Fretheim, *The Suffering of God; An Old Testament Perspective* (Philadelphia: Fortress, 1984), p. 123.

4 Council of Chalcedon (A.D. 451) http://www.newadvent.org/fathers/3811.htm

5 Westminster Confession of Faith (A.D. 1646) http://www.reformed.org/documents/wcf_with_proofs/

6 G. Walter Hansen, *The Emotions of Jesus*, Christianity Today, Feb. 3, 1997, Vol. 41, No. 2.

7 Dennis Ngien, *The God Who Suffers,* Christianity Today, Feb. 3, 1997, Vol. 41, No. 2.

8 Marcel Sarot, *God, Emotions, and Corporality: A Thomist Perspective,* University of Utrecht, The Netherlands.

9 Ronald Goetz, *The Suffering God: The Rise of a New Orthodoxy,* Christian Century, April 16, 1986, p.385.

10 Raymond C. Ortlund, Jr., *God's Unfaithful Wife, New Studies in Biblical Theology* (Westmont: IVP Academic, 2016), Kindle.

11 Ibid.

[12] Paul Copan. *Is God a Moral Monster? Making Sense of the Old Testament God.* (Ada: Baker Books, 2011), Kindle.

[13] David Wilkerson. *The Queen in Gold! The Bride of Christ.* Times Square Church website [online].

[14] Ibid.

[15] Michael L. Brown, Paul W. Ferris, *Jeremiah, Lamentations, The Expositor's Bible Commentary* (Grand Rapids: Zondervan Academic, 2017), Kindle.

[16] Ibid.

[17] Ibid.

[18] Walter A. Elwell, *Baker Encyclopedia of the Bible, Volumes 1 and 2* (Ada: Baker Pub Group, 1988), Kindle.

[19] A.B. Simpson, *Days of Heaven on Earth: A Daily Devotional to Comfort and Inspire* (Chicago: Moody Publishers, 1984), Kindle.

[20] Timothy Keller, *Counterfeit Gods* (London: Penguin Books, 2011), Kindle.

[21] Os Guinness and John Steel, *No God But God* (Chicago: Moody 1992), p. 31.

[22] *Faithlife Study Bible,* Copyright 2021 Faithlife, LLC, Makers of Logos Bible Software. Http:///www.logos.com.

[23] David Clarkson. *Soul Idolatry Excludes Men Out of Heaven.* (Mangatangi: Titus Books, 2014), Kindle.

[24] Kyle Idleman, *Gods at War, Defeating the Idols that Battle for Your Heart* (Grand Rapids: Zondervan, 2018), Kindle.

[25] John Calvin. Christian Classics Ethereal Library https://www.ccel.org › ccel › calvin › institutes.toc.html.

[26] Kyle Idleman, *Gods at War, Defeating the Idols that Battle for Your Heart* (Grand Rapids: Zondervan, 2018), Kindle.

[27] Timothy Keller. *Counterfeit Gods.* (London: Penguin Books, 2011), Kindle.

[28] Blaise Pascal, cited in *12,000 Religious Quotations, Compiled and Edited by Frank S. Mead* (Grand Rapids: Baker, 1989), p. 243.

[29] John White, *Money Isn't God* (Downers Grove: Intervarsity, 1993), p. 53.

[30] Raymond C. Ortlund, Jr., *God's Unfaithful Wife, New Studies in Biblical Theology* (Westmont: IVP Academic, 2016), Kindle.

[31] Acts 8:20 - Peter said to him, "Your money perish with you, because you thought that the gift of God could be purchased with money!"

[32] Michael Brown, *Go And Sin No More* (Ventura: Regal, 1999), pp. 115-116.

[33] Kyle Idleman, *Gods at War, Defeating the Idols that Battle for Your Heart* (Grand Rapids: Zondervan, 2018), Kindle.

[34] David Clarkson. *Soul Idolatry Excludes Men Out of Heaven* (Mangatangi: Titus Books, 2014), Kindle.

[35] Francis Frangipane, *From Hollywood To Holywood,* http://www.etpv.org/ 2004/fhoho.html

[36] Paul Johansson, *The Idol of Vision,* Kairos Magazine, March-April 2006.

[37] Judson Cornwall, *Things We Adore* (Shippensburg, PA: Destiny, 1991), p. 31.

[38] Andy Comiskey, *Pursuing Sexual Wholeness* (Lake Mary: Creation House, 1989), p. 102.

[39] Baltasar Gracian y Morales, cited in 12,000 *Religious Quotations, Compiled and Edited by Frank S. Mead* (Grand Rapids: Baker, 1989), p. 243.

[40] Dr. Carl Ellis, Jr.. *What Happens When Politics Drive Our Faith?* Online Article at https://rts.edu/resources/what- happens-when-politics-drive-our-faith/

[41] Timothy Keller. *Counterfeit Gods*. (London: Penguin Books, 2011), Kindle.

[42] Rick Joyner, Quoted in Jeremiah Johnson, *The Altar* (Shippensburg: Destiny Image), Kindle.

[43] https://bibleportal.com/bible-quotes/author/Corrie-Ten-Boom

[44] Warren Weirsbe, *Real Worship* (Nashville: Oliver - Nelson Books, 1986), Kindle.

[45] Richard Cecil, cited in *12,000 Religious Quotations, Compiled and Edited by Frank S. Mead* (Grand Rapids: Baker, 1989), p. 399.

[46] A.W. Tozer, *Man, the Dwelling Place of God* (Camp Hill: Christian Publications, 1976), p. 71.

[47] Samuel Rutherford, *Extracts from the Letters of Samuel Rutherford*, Published by the Central Bible Truth Depot. Online https://www.stempublishing.com/authors/smith/RUTHRFRD.html.

[48] Judson Cornwall, *Things We Adore* (Shippensburg: Destiny Image, 1991), p. 142.

[49] Thomas Chalmers, *The Expulsive Power of a New Affection.* (Louisville: GLH Publishing), Kindle.

[50] Ed Welch, *Addictions: A Banquet in the Grave.* (Greensboro: New Growth Press, 2012), Kindle.

[51] David Wilkerson, *The Cross and the Switchblade* (New York: Berkley, 1986), Kindle.

[52] Timothy Keller, *Counterfeit Gods* (London: Penguin Books, 2011), Kindle.

[53] Charles Spurgeon, *Spurgeon's Sermons on Soulwinning* (Grand Rapids: Kregel Publications, 1995), p. 50.

[54] George H. Guthrie, *James, Revised Expositor's Bible Commentary* (Grand Rapids: Zondervan, 2006), p. 727.

[55] Paul Copan, *Is God a Moral Monster? Making Sense of the Old Testament God* (Grand Rapids: Baker Publishing Group), Kindle.

[56] Raymond C. Ortlund, Jr., *God's Unfaithful Wife, New Studies in Biblical Theology* (Westmont: IVP Academic, 2016), Kindle.

[57] Definition of Grace. *Strong's Greek Dictionary of the New Testament.*

[58] Charles L. Allen. *God's Psychiatry.* (Ada: Revell, 1984), Kindle.

[59] Raymond C. Ortlund, Jr. *God's Unfaithful Wife (New Studies in Biblical Theology).* InterVarsity Press. Kindle Edition.

[60] https://www.gospeltruth.net/Wrightbio/finneybi.html.

[61] Jonathan Edwards. *Works of Jonathan Edwards.* https://ccel.org/ccel/edwards/works1/works1.viii.ii.html.

[62] Michael L. Brown. *FIRE School of Ministry NYC, sermon notes,* 2006.

[63] Phillip Brooks, cited in *12,000 Religious Quotations, Compiled and Edited by Frank S. Mead* (Grand Rapids: Baker, 1989), p. 51.

[64] Matthew Henry, *Commentary on the Whole Bible, Vol. 4, Isaiah to Malachi* (New York: Hendrickson Publishers, 2003), p. 888.

[65] Revelation 19:7-8, 21:5 The marriage of the Lamb has come, and His wife has made herself ready. And to her it was granted to be arrayed in fine linen, clean and bright, for the fine linen is the righteous acts of the saints… And He said to me, "Write, for these words are true and faithful."

[66] G. R. Beasley-Murray, *The Book of Revelation: Based on the Revised Standard Version* (Eugene: Wipf and Stock, 2010).

[67] Jeremiah Johnson. *The Altar.* (Shippensburg: Destiny Image, 2022), Kindle.

[68] James Strong. *Strong's Bible Concordance: Including Holy Bible - King James Edition. (E-artnow, 2021), Kindle.*

[69] Orville James Nave. *Nave's Topical Bible Concordance.* (TruthBeTold Ministry, 2017), Kindle.

[70] Dictionary-Definitions from Oxford Languages. https://languages.oup.com/google-dictionary-en/

[71] A. W. Tozer, *Worship, The Missing Jewel* (Camp Hill: Christian Publications, 1992), p. 24.

[72] Ibid.

[73] Eric Gilmour, *The School of His Presence* (CreateSpace, 2017), Kindle.

74 Brian Simmons, *Song of Songs: Divine Romance* (Savage: Broadstreet Publishing Group, 2020), Kindle.

75 Augustine. *The Complete Works of St. Augustine* (2019), Kindle.

76 https://www.christianquotes.info/quotes-by-author/richard-j-foster-quotes/

77 https://www.logos.com/grow/31-of-j-i-packer-best-quotes/

78 James MacDonald. *Vertical Church: What Every Heart Longs for. What Every Church Can Be.* (Colorado Springs: David C. Cook), Kindle.

79 Charles Spurgeon. The Feast of the Lord. https://www.spurgeon.org/resource-library/sermons/the-feast-of-the-lord/#flipbook/

80 Raymond C. Ortlund, Jr., *God's Unfaithful Wife, New Studies in Biblical Theology* (Westmont: IVP Academic, 2016), Kindle.

81 Ibid.

82 BibleAsk Team. *What does the Latter Rain mean?* https://bibleask.org/what-is-the-meaning-of-the-latter-rain/

83 Charles Simpson. *Walking in the Footsteps of David Wilkerson.* (Shippensburg: Destiny Image, 2018), Kindle.

84 *O Come, Let Us Adore Him,* by John Francis Wade, https://hymnary.org/text/o_come_let_us_adore_him

ALSO AVAILABLE FROM BRIDGE-LOGOS

THE JEREMIAH CODE

Don Wilkerson

This is one of the most well-known promises of God. A promise given to the Prophet directly from the Lord. This promise is for everyone, it gives believers encouragement and non-believers a reason to come to know the Lord.

Pastor Don Wilkerson endeavors to unwrap the meaning of passage 29:11 in greater depth, not just for those who may have relapsed, but for all who know the verse, and for those hearing it for the first time.

This book will bring to life the passage and will give those who have relapsed back into alcoholism and drug addiction, after a period of recovery, a new hope.

29:11 is one of the most powerful promises that restoration is possible for everyone. *God said it is so!*

ISBN: 978-1-61036-278-8

ALSO AVAILABLE FROM BRIDGE-LOGOS